Brander Matthews

The Theatres of Paris

Brander Matthews

The Theatres of Paris

ISBN/EAN: 9783337428495

Printed in Europe, USA, Canada, Australia, Japan

Cover: Foto ©ninafisch / pixelio.de

More available books at **www.hansebooks.com**

THE

THEATRES OF PARIS

BY

J. BRANDER MATTHEWS

WITH ILLUSTRATIONS

AFTER

MADRAZO, CAROLUS DURAN, GAUCHEREL, SARAH BERNHARDT,
AND OTHERS.

NEW YORK
CHARLES SCRIBNER'S SONS
743 AND 745 BROADWAY
1880

À
M. C. COQUELIN
de la Comédie-Française :

SOUVENIR DES SOIRÉES PASSÉES DANS SA LOGE.

J. B. M.

PREFACE.

GOOD Americans, we are told, when they die go to Paris. It is to be feared that a many of the few bad ones who may exist take time by the forelock, and spend their days and nights in Paris now, alive and in the flesh. As a guide to both these classes of my countrymen this little book is intended. It is meant for the reader who—to use Mr. Lowell's apt phrase—has travelled only at his own fireside, as well as for the reader who is wont often to cross the water.

The title is taken from a short article on the Theatres of Paris, presented in the *Art Journal* last fall. From this article, as well as from others contributed to *Scribner's*, *Lippincott's*, and *Appleton's* Magazines, and to the *Nation*, I have not hesitated to borrow freely now and then whatever might aid me in the composition of the following chapters.

Special acknowledgment should be made of the assistance derived from M. Charles Nuitter's book on "Le Nouvel Opéra" (Paris, 1875), and from M. Francisque Sarcey's series of histrionic monographs "Comédiens et Comédiennes" (Paris, 1876-1880). For the chapters on the Comédie-Française, both information and illustrations have been taken from M. Sarcey's invaluable volumes. For the portrait of M. Coquelin, after Madrazo, I am indebted to a recent number of the *Moliériste*—an excellent monthly magazine, devoted wholly to the study of the noble humorist who is the glory of French dramatic literature.

J. B. M.

NEW YORK, March, 1880.

CONTENTS.

	PAGE
CHAPTER I.—INTRODUCTION	1
" II.—THE ACADEMY OF MUSIC	17
" III.—THE NEW OPÉRA	39
" IV.—THE OTHER MUSICAL THEATRES	60
" V.—THE COMÉDIE-FRANÇAISE	71
" VI.—THE ACTRESSES OF THE COMÉDIE-FRANÇAISE	89
" VII.—THE ACTORS OF THE COMÉDIE-FRANÇAISE	114
" VIII.—THE THÉÂTRE FRANÇAIS	136
" IX.—THE OTHER COMEDY THEATRES	154
" X.—THE THEATRES OF DRAMA AND SPECTACLE	167
" XI.—THE THEATRES OF FARCE AND EXTRAVAGANZA	182
" XII.—OTHER PLACES OF AMUSEMENT	190
" XIII.—CONCLUSION	200

LIST OF ILLUSTRATIONS.

	PAGE
THE NEW OPÉRA	Frontispiece
THE AVENUE DE L'OPÉRA	18
THE GRAND STAIRCASE	43
THE GRAND FOYER	47
THE RENAISSANCE	67
COQUELIN (AFTER GAUCHEREL)	79
FEBVRE (AFTER GAUCHEREL)	83
SARAH-BERNHARDT (AFTER GAUCHEREL)	93
SARAH-BERNHARDT (SKETCHED BY HERSELF)	95
SOPHIE CROIZETTE (AFTER THE PAINTING BY CAROLUS DURAN)	103
MARIA FAVART (AFTER GAUCHEREL)	111
GOT (AFTER GAUCHEREL)	117
DELAUNAY (AFTER GAUCHEREL)	125
MOUNET-SULLY (AFTER GAUCHEREL)	129
WORMS (AFTER GAUCHEREL)	133
THE THÉÂTRE FRANÇAIS	137
COQUELIN (AFTER MADRAZO'S PAINTING)	145
THE ODÉON	158
THE VAUDEVILLE	161
THE PORTE ST. MARTIN	169
THE CHÂTELET	179

THE THEATRES OF PARIS.

CHAPTER I.

INTRODUCTION.

IN the fulness, strength, and originality of its dramatic literature, France has for fifty years stood alone among the nations of Europe; and in the number of its theatres, in the excellence of its actors, and in the careful splendor of its theatrical performances, Paris is the first among the cities of the world.

The Parisians are essentially a theatrical people; their talk and their tastes are theatrical—and at times even their actions are theatrical. A new play by a well-known author is an event. It is a nine days' topic. It is criticised, written about and written against, abused and praised, seen and heard by all Paris. Sometimes, like the "Rabagas" of M. Sardou, it is a political pamphlet; then it is applauded and hissed at once; the police are always present; there may be nightly disturbances; and there is constant fear of a riot. Sometimes, like the "Femme de Claude" of M. Alexandre Dumas the younger, it treats a social evil, attacking it with a daring, unconventional pen; then it is heard in silence and discussed with acrimony. Sometimes, like the "Balsamo" of the two Dumas, a play expected to cause a great sensation fails, and sinks at once beneath the wave of oblivion. Sometimes on the eve of production it is forbidden by the censors; then the author immediately prints it for all Paris to read, and the censors are either scolded or laughed at. The interdict laid on the piece remains until the censors change their minds, or the nation changes its government. Permission being finally given to produce the play, the forbidden fruit is tasted by the palates of the Parisians, and it is generally found to be over-ripe; for it has been kept too long.

This Parisian predilection for the theatre and frank recognition of the importance of the stage is of no recent growth. The populace thronged to the miracle-plays of the early brethren; Corneille was induced to compose the "Cid" as an attack on Richelieu's policy; the Cardinal himself wrote tragedies; Molière was sustained against the attacks of the clerical bigots by Louis XIV.; Beaumarchais's "Barber of Seville" may have hastened the rising of the people; the theatres were crowded during the Revolution; and Napoleon dated a decree about the Théâtre Français from Moscow. In a work on dramatic art, published in 1772, M.

de Cailhava, one of the dramatists of that day, says:

"A new piece is advertised, all Paris flies there; the curtain rises, the actors appear, the friends of the author applaud, the enemies of his person or his talent hawk or blow their noses. They go to supper; those of the guests who could not be present in the theatre, ask about the success of the novelty. 'Tis pitiable, or 'tis delicious, says a *merveilleux*, who in his life never judged anything but by contagion. From the end of the table a pretty woman confirms his judgment, only adding that the hair of the actress was very badly dressed." *Tempora mutantur*, but might not this paragraph have been written in this year of grace 1880? It is not only in France, alas, that people are prone to judge by contagion.

The desire to be present at the first performance of a new piece has but deepened with the lapse of years. Upon the announcement of the name of the play and the date of its birth, the author is besieged with applications for seats. His relatives, his friends, his enemies, those who know him, those who do not know him, even those who have never heard of him, all signify their anxiety to be present at the first night of his new piece. And, as M. Dumas warns us, woe betide him if he accede to the requests thus made, if he fill the house with his enemies, his friends, or his family! The piece will fail! It was not played before the proper audience. It was not seen by the three hundred people who arrogate to themselves the title of "all Paris." These men of letters and men of the world, these strangers, artists, and critics, these ladies of good society and bad, these bankers and do-nothings about town, do not care whether the play be good or bad, whether it be tragedy or opéra bouffe—they only want to be present in their proper places at its first performance; they only want to hear it; they will see whether it be good or bad; they will judge it, and their judgment will be final. If this "all Paris" disapprove of a drama; if it fail upon its first performance before this mixed, indiscriminating, and yet critical audience—its doom is sealed. It may be eulogized by the critics, but it can never hope to hold a lasting place on the stage, and—it will never make money! Rash is the writer who, afraid of this public or ignorant of its power, seeks to avoid its verdict. His piece is fated. If on its first night "all Paris" be not present, and if the play does not find favor in their eyes, it cannot be good.

M. Dumas, in a witty article on first performances in Paris, tells an anecdote in point. A Russian nobleman, long resident in France, and a friend of M. Dumas's, wrote a comedy, which was accepted and produced at the Gymnase Theatre. The author, holding a high social position, bought up every seat, invited his titled friends; the countess, the duchess, the baroness filled box and balcony; the *Almanach de Gotha* crowded the theatre. And the play—a charming comedy not unworthy of Scribe—fell flat. Why? Because, said M. Dumas, the author knew how to compose his piece, but not how to compose his house. Whereupon the noble Russian returned to St. Petersburg, saying to M. Dumas, " Decidedly it is too difficult to be a Parisian !"

Before taking up the theatres of the capital of France, one after another, let us consider the physiognomy of a Parisian playhouse. The theatres of Paris are very unlike those of New York, but they are so like each other that a description of one will answer for nearly all the others. From the proscenium arch, broad enough to hold two boxes in each tier, stretch three or more semi-oval or horseshoe galleries, built almost directly over each other, and not receding as is the custom in American theatres. The body of the ground floor is filled with orchestra chairs, to which formerly ladies were not admitted. Now, however, except at the Théâtre Français, the Odéon, the Opéra Comique, and the Palais Royal, this Salic law has been abrogated, and the fair sex may sit where it likes. Behind the orchestra chairs is the pit, which extends back only to the first galleries, under which, on the ground floor, is a semicircular tier of dark boxes called *baignoires*, or bathrooms, and the heat of Parisian theatres makes the name not inappropriate. The first balcony as a rule contains two or three rows of chairs, backed by a row of boxes; the second tier is generally all small boxes; the third, given up entirely to benches, corresponds to our family circle. Sometimes there is a fourth gallery, named the amphitheatre, and nicknamed the paradise most aptly, for it is inhabited by the "gods," or perhaps, as the younger M. Dumas has wittily put it, "because they eat apples there."

Scattered along the boulevards are four or five ticket offices, containing not a map but a model of each theatre, so that the purchaser of a ticket can see at a glance his future position. Strange to say, following a short-sighted custom, the price of seats, if bought in advance either at one of these agencies or at the theatre itself, is higher than when the doors are open. An orchestra chair at the Théâtre Français costs six francs if purchased at the gate just as you enter the theatre at night, and eight if chosen during the day. At the Opéra the same seat costs ten or twelve francs.

These prices do not differ greatly from those which we pay in America, but when we allow for the greater purchasing power of money in Europe, we see at once that prices are decidedly higher there than they are here. And in all that conduces to material comfort, the theatres of New York are far superior to those of Paris. In fact, the playhouses of Paris, even the best of them, are very uncomfortable. The seats are narrow, hard, and stiff; the aisles are not wide, and are frequently filled up with little folding-chairs. There is no mode of rapid egress in case of fire. There is little or no ventilation. To relieve the pressure on your legs, cribbed, cabined, and confined in very close quarters, you can hire a footstool from one of the aged hags who act as ushers. For this boon you are expected to pay half a franc. If you wish a bill of the play, that also must be purchased.

If, however, the Parisian manager has not shown himself solicitous for the comfort of his customers, he has at least endeavored in one way to save them trouble. The spectator in Paris is not called on to applaud. Never mind how much he may be pleased with the performance, he need not rend his gloves or make his hands tingle in the effort to express his approbation. He may rest sure that the salaried applauders of the theatre, detailed for regular service every night, will do their duty, and enliven the evening's entertainment with the regulation rounds of applause.

In the front row of the pit, immediately behind the orchestra chairs, sit the *claque*, as the hirelings who thunder forth the repeated salvos are called, marshalled under the eye of the "contractor for success," as the chief of the band grandiloquently styles himself. It is only the chief and two or three picked hands who come to the theatre every night; the rest are volunteers picked up each evening and doing their share of the applause under the orders of the chief, in return for a chance to see the play gratis. A humble-minded man, of broad palms and liberal views, by a little manœuvring may thus manage to see every play in Paris for nothing. One finds the *claque* everywhere, except of late at the Opéra and the Théâtre Français. At these two houses it was found possible to dispense with it during the rush and excitement of the Exhibition of 1878, and the experiment having succeeded then, the hireling bravos have not yet returned.

The *claque* is autocratic and intolerant; like true Frenchmen, the members of it know their own importance, and are inclined to regard themselves as public functionaries. A characteristic letter is in circulation, written to Rachel by a chief of the *claque*, who had heard that she was dissatisfied with the applause she had received on the second performance of a successful piece: "Mademoiselle, I cannot remain under the obloquy of a reproach from lips such as yours! The following is an authentic statement of what really took place: At the first representation I led the attack in person no less than thirty-three times! We had three acclamations, four hilarities, two thrilling movements, four renewals of applause, and two indefinite explosions. In fact, to such an extent did we carry our applause that the occupants of the stalls were scandalized, and cried out, 'Turn them out!' My men were positively overcome with fatigue, and intimated to me that they could not again go through such an evening. Seeing such to be the case, I applied for the manuscript, and, after having profoundly studied the piece, I was obliged to make up my mind, for the second representation, to certain curtailments in the service of my men. I, however, applied them only to MM. —— ——; and, 'if the temporary office which I hold affords me the opportunity, I will make them ample amends. In such a situation as that which I have just depicted, I have only to request you to believe firmly in my profound admiration and respectful zeal; and I venture to entreat you to have some consideration for the difficulties which environ me.—I am, mademoiselle," etc.

The spirit of a performance in Paris really does in a great measure depend on the *claque*. Having had the matter so long taken out of their hands, the people (except upon rare occasions) seem to have forgotten how to applaud. Now applause is necessary to the actor. It gives encouragement, and, as Mrs. Siddons said, "better still—breath!" Hired approbation is better than none at all. There is a curious anecdote, at once pertinent to this, and peculiar in its revelation of a great artist's whims.

Once after playing one of his best creations in a minor theatre, Frédérick Lemaître was not called before the curtain after one of his finest bursts of passion. Indignant and impudent, the actor caused the curtain to be raised, and walking to the centre of the stage in front of the footlights, he asked if M. Jules was present. No one answering, he then demanded M. Auguste. Nor was there any response to this either. "Gentlemen," said the actor, "I have been cheated—robbed! I paid those two fellows twenty francs apiece to call me before the curtain to-night; and they have not done it."

Although Parisian play-goers have seemingly abandoned the privilege of applauding a good performance, they have not surrendered the right to hiss a bad one. This right is sometimes exercised gently and wittily, as was the case in the last century when the heroine of Marmontel's tragedy of "Cleopatra" clasped upon her arm a mechanical asp of cunning workmanship, devised by Vaucanson, and the venomous beast reared its head, and before plunging its apparent fangs into the arm of the actress, hissed shrilly; whereupon a spectator arose and went out with the simple remark, "I agree with the asp." More generally in our day the hissing is done vigorously. In a hit at the times, called "1867," produced at the Porte St. Martin, Mlle. Silly was roundly hissed for a parody on her intimate enemy Mlle. Schneider; and a few weeks later Mlle. Delval, Mlle. Silly's statuesque sister, appeared as *Truth*, robed only in her innocence and a halo of electric light, a clothing deemed inadequate by the audience, and so she too was hissed. On both these occasions the *claque* frantically applauded, trying in vain to hide the hisses; and when the police in the theatre turned the hissers out, the audience refused to allow the play to go on until the ejected spectators were permitted to return.

The French law, while recognizing the right of the paying spectator to express his disapproval, if the goods he has purchased are not what he had been led to expect, will not allow any cabal or conspiracy, and forbids disturbance of any kind except while the curtain is up. So long as the green cloth shuts out the stage, all must be decorum. In Paris the boisterousness of the Dublin gallery boy could never be tolerated. The Parisians would have been amazed at an incident which is told in the history of the Irish stage. When Sophocles' tragedy of "Antigone" was produced at the Theatre Royal, with Mendelssohn's music, the gallery gods were greatly pleased, and, according to their custom, demanded a sight of the author. "Bring out Sapherclaze," they yelled. The manager explained that Sophocles had been dead two thousand years and more, and could not well come. Thereat a small voice shouted from the gallery, "Then chuck us out his mummy."

Like almost everything in France, the theatres are ruled by rigid laws. There is a duly prescribed way of building a theatre and of isolating its scenery from all chance of conflagration. The scene-room must never be in a building contiguous to the theatre, and so it is no unusual sight in Paris to see immense carts carrying the painted parlors, and porticos, and forests, and firesides of the stage through the streets from the theatre to the scenic storehouse and back again, as occasion serves. A detail of firemen and of police is always on duty at the theatre. During the performance there must be present a physician, to whose use a special seat is reserved, known to all the officials of the theatre. Nor does the parental care of the government confine itself to the interior of the house; it also provides for the exterior. It even prescribes the method of bill-posting.

In their theory of advertising, the theatres of Paris, judged from an American point of view, are miserably defective. There are no "mammoth bills" to be seen in Paris; no "streamers;" no "gutter-snipes;" none of the pictorial printing which is the pride of an enterprising American speculator. Special permission had to be asked and obtained in 1867 before the gorgeous hues of the many-colored posters, brought across the ocean by the American circus, were allowed to be displayed before the wondering eyes of the Parisian populace. In the same year Mr. Sothern ran over to the French capital to show the Parisians the " American Cousin " (admirably acted by Mr. John T. Raymond), and to announce his coming he caused life-size heads of *Lord Dundreary,* eyeglass and whiskers and all, to be stuck up wherever space offered; and the surprised Parisians went around asking one another who " the man with the eyeglass " might be?

Instead of all this—and even a patriotic American can but acknowledge that the custom is more quietly artistic and probably quite as effective—the bills of all the theatres, of a given size prescribed by law (about fifteen inches broad by thirty high), are printed together and displayed on posts in the principal streets and boulevards, as well as on an occasional dead wall. The announcements are printed in black on colored backgrounds, the hue varying for each theatre, thus making a curious parti-color effect. Any sudden change in the programme must be notified to the public by a white band pasted across the original advertisement. No theatre can post a bill all white, as that color is reserved for the official announcements of the state.

By these regulations the government does no real harm to the theatres; it may even benefit them in so far as it restricts the competition in bill-posting, which is at times wellnigh ruinous to an American manager. But the interference of the government is not always so beneficent. For example, it takes one-tenth of the gross receipts of every theatre in Paris for the benefit of the poor of the city. Again and again have the managers tried to obtain the repeal of this obnoxious tax, but as yet in vain.

When the theatre-goer in Paris enters the door and presents his ticket, that document is not glanced at hastily by a single gateman, as in New York, but critically examined by three grave officials who consider it carefully. One of these three is the ticket-taker of the theatre; the second is the government envoy, who sees that a correct statement of the gross receipts is made up, so that the poor may get their tithe; and the third is the agent of the Society of Dramatic Authors and Composers, who also verifies the gross receipts, so that the author may not be defrauded of any of his dues.

Space fails in this little volume to tell at length of the hooks of steel by which the powerful association of the dramatic authors has bound to itself the managers of France. The old country manager who liked to give Shakespeare's plays, because the author could not "come to the treasury asking for money," would be greatly displeased in France to find that, however old the play, and however dead the copyright, the agents of the society would still collect the proportionate fee, although in this case only to turn it over to a charitable fund for the relief of the theatrical poor. The dramatist in France is paid a certain percentage of the nightly receipts; it may vary from ten to fifteen *per cent.* according to the importance and classification of the theatre. When, as is generally the case, there is more than one piece acted on the same evening, the authors divide their percentage of the receipts in proportion to the length of the plays of each.

The Society of the Dramatic Authors and Composers contains every dramatic author of France. It is therefore in effect a monopoly; and it rules managers with a rod of iron. It makes a contract with each manager, specifying what proportion of his receipts the society shall take. If he refuse to sign the contract, the society forbids any of its members to allow any of their plays to be acted in his theatre. This step practically closes his doors, for he has nothing to act except translations from foreign languages — which the Parisian play-goer does not care for—and old pieces on which the copyright has run out—which the Parisian play-goer has probably seen until he is tired. So in the end the manager accepts the proffered contract. There is then no haggling about terms. The young author never need fear being beaten down, and the dramatic veteran never can doubt the certainty of payment. The society collects the royalty and holds it, subject to the author's order.. The manager dare not attempt to pay even the freshest novice less than the percentage agreed upon, and to secure a favorite writer he very often offers to pay more.

The Opéra alone is exempt from this payment of a percentage of its gross receipts. It pays instead a fixed sum of five hundred francs a night, to be divided between the author and composer, whatever may be its receipts.

CHAPTER II.

THE ACADEMY OF MUSIC.

IN the very centre of modern Paris, in a broad and ample space, cleared expressly for the more abundant display of its gorgeous coloring and lofty proportions, stands the magnificent monument which France has erected in its capital to honor and to house the union of music and the drama. Seen of all men who may pass through the city by the Seine, and situated in the midst of what is called the American quarter, as though to extort by dint of boldness the admiration of all transatlantic wanderers, the Opéra bears witness to the high esteem in which the Parisian people hold the three fine arts closely akin one to another—acting and singing and dancing.

Even the streets around this temple of the muses lend their testimony also to show how highly Paris appreciates those who have contributed in a great degree to its intellectual enjoyment, and aided in the attainment of the artistic preëminence it claims over other cities. In other parts of the city are an Avenue Molière and a Boulevard Beaumarchais, and here, around the new home of the institution they did so much to lift above all its rivals, are streets bearing the names of Meyerbeer, Halévy, Auber, and Scribe. And from the Opéra to the Théâtre Français, linking the two great histrionic institutions of the nation, runs a noble street, recently cut, and called the Avenue de l'Opéra.

THE AVENUE DE L'OPÉRA.

As the National Academy of Music—for such is the official style and title of the theatre which every Parisian calls simply the Opéra—is the most prominent of all places of amusement in France, from its ancient and honorable history, as well as from its sumptuous and flamboyant habitation, it is fit that any description of the theatres of Paris should begin with some account of what was for long, even if it be no longer, the first musical theatre of the world.

The opera has always been a royal, imperial, or national institution; even in these days of heavy taxation, the republic allots it a substantial annual subvention of nearly a million of francs. According to Voltaire, France owes her comedy and her opera to two cardinals. The assertion is not absolutely accurate, for while Richelieu was of material assistance to the earlier dramatists, credit is due to Mazarin only for suggestion. The success of a company of Italian singers, imported by the cardinal to please Anne of Austria, incited the Abbé Perrin to produce, in 1659, the " Pastorale d'Issy," with music by Cambert. Mazarin was disposed to encourage the new enterprise, but he died in 1661, and it was not until 1669 that Perrin received a royal patent according him a monopoly of the opera. This was soon revoked in favor of Lulli, a wily little Italian, who is popularly believed to be the originator of French opera. Lulli, at one time a scullion, and then the head of a band of violinists, first attracted the attention of the king in one of Molière's pieces, for which he had composed the music, and was at last emboldened, by the aid of Madame Montespan, to open the Opéra in May, 1672, with a pastoral into which he had woven his musical interludes from the " Bourgeois Gentilhomme" and "Georges Dandin." The next year Molière died, and by royal command Lulli took possession of the great humorist's more commodious theatre, thus ousting Molière's widow and her fellow-actors, just as he had previously supplanted Perrin. Lulli was versatile and industrious, and when he died, in 1687, he left behind him nineteen operas (not counting ballets and interludes), and six hundred and thirty thousand golden livres.

And whatever his personal failings, it can scarcely be denied that he was of great and lasting benefit to the opera. To his personal influence was due the royal favor which sustained the new enterprise in its helpless infancy. So much was it petted by the court and patronized by the king, that the nobility thought it no disgrace to appear in person and sing on its stage. In royal letters-patent of the date of 1672, one may read that, "We wish and it pleases Us, that all gentlemen and damsels" (*damoiselles*) "should sing in the pieces and representations of our Royal Academy of Music, without its being supposed that they detract from their title of nobility, or from their privileges, duties, rights, and immunities."

To Lulli also is due the development of dramatic dancing. Although the ballet had a footing at the Opéra before his reign, there were no female dancers, the women characters being taken by boys. As we all know, the same custom obtained in the English theatres in Shakespeare's day. Lulli reformed this altogether. In 1681 he brought out " The Triumph of Love " (a ballet which, at court, had found favor in the eyes of the king) at the Opéra, with four female dancers, the first professional *ballerine* of which we have record. One of these, Mademoiselle Lafontaine, " a beautiful and stylish dancer," says Durey de Noinville, was so successful that she was hailed as the " queen of the dance."

During the next hundred years there is but little of interest to record in the history of the Opéra, excepting only the often-described quarrel between the partisans of Glück and of Piccini. But in 1781 there occurred an instance of royal generosity well worthy of record. The theatre in the Palais Royal, in which the Opéra had been established for ninety years, was burnt, and, under the patronage of Marie Antoinette, the architect, Lenoir, by working day and night, built a new opera-house at the Porte St. Martin in eighty-six days. Rumors at once began to circulate at court that it was unsafe—that a building erected in such hot haste could not have been properly constructed. The intimidated authorities therefore decided that, in order to test the strength of the new opera-house before permitting the queen to enter it, a performance should be given gratis to the people of Paris. The beams having been thus tested by the common herd, their majesties honored the Opéra with their presence. And the building thus hastily erected long survives the departure of the Opéra from within its walls, for, like the line of kings which encouraged its first steps, the National Academy of Music has been a migratory institution, and has moved twelve times from its foundation to the day when it took possession of its thirteenth home, the present opera-house, occupied by it only within the last half decade.

In 1791, for the first time, the names of the singers appeared in the bill of the play. Previously it had been understood that the best singers appeared on Fridays only. Three years later, when the Opéra was transferred to the building confiscated by fraud from Mlle. Montansier, the spectators in the pit were at last provided with seats. The year before this, under the Terror, on March 20, 1793, Mozart's "Marriage of Figaro" was performed for the first time. The vacillating Louis XVI., after absolutely interdicting Beaumarchais's piece, at length authorized its performance, and finally acted in it himself with his queen. His predecessor, Louis XIV., had danced in ballets, and his successor, Louis XVIII., when Count of Provence, was the anonymous author of more than one opera libretto, notably of the "Caravan of Cairo," set by Grétry.

This composer did not long retain his royalist tastes. During the troublous times of '93 and the succeeding years of the republic over two thousand revolutionary dramas were written; more than half of them were acted, and the stage of the National Academy of Music did not fail to have its share; and in the archives stored away in the capacious galleries of the new building are the scores of many revolutionary operas by Grétry, Méhul, and Rouget de l'Isle, in which the representatives of the people—municipal officers girt with their tricolored scarfs, or sans-culottes curates—replace the gods of Olympus as the *dei ex machinâ*. In these curious works we find the new-born Goddess of Reason dancing the Carmagnole, or singing the Ça Ira, a revolutionary song of particular interest to Americans, for it was suggested by a remark of Franklin's. The Goddess of Reason was the wife of the bookseller Momoro. The Goddess of Liberty was the beautiful Mlle. Maillard of the Opéra, who had so often played the part in the "Offering to Liberty," that at last it became incarnated in her. The people, giving a local habitation to their ideal, no longer distinguished the actress from the goddess. In spite of her unconcealed royalist sympathies, she was constrained to personate Liberty in all the civic celebrations, and even to be adored in the "Temple of Reason" (formerly Notre Dame), together with Mme. Ducamp and Mlle. Florigny, also of the Opéra, as Equality and Fraternity.

This "Offrande à la Liberté" and a kindred piece, "La Rosière Républicaine," were the two great successes of a new school of high-flown and hybrid ballet-operas, half dancing and half singing. Other and more regular ballets fared badly; revolutions are bad times for the fine arts. Three times was the money appropriated for a patriotic ballet composed by Gardel on so revolutionary a subject as "William Tell," and three times was the money stolen before it could reach the composer. It was only clap-trap and blood-and-thunder pieces, full of sound and fury and signifying nothing, which could hope for a hearing on the stage of the Opéra. And of these there was no lack. The National Academy of Music turned itself into the illustrated supplement of the daily newspaper, reflecting the lurid glare of the "latest from the seat of war."

Battle after battle was repeated on the stage of the Opéra, after the news of the reality had come from the borders of France. The rapidly-succeeding events of the last ten years of the century were often mirrored behind the curtain of the Opéra. In this a precedent was followed. Twenty years before, the Opéra had brought out "Mirza," a ballet in three acts, setting on the stage the events of the American Revolution, in which the soldiers of France were then fighting side by side with the Continentals of these colonies. Let us imagine, if haply we can, the figure cut by the dignified Washington and "Grandison-Cromwell" Lafayette as they pirouetted in a minuet with grave reserve! A few years later, America again appears on the stage of the Opéra in " L'Embarras de Richesses," a ballet by Grétry, in which the four quarters of the world were seen—America dancing "a minuet of the time of Pericles."

During the whole Revolution the stage of the Opéra was prompt to set forth the shifting scenes of blood and iron; and every victory over the foreign foe was at once set to music and represented before the footlights. Indeed the Opéra had a direct connection with the first great event of the Revolution: its property-room had been sacked of its sabres to assist in arming the populace for the assault on the Bastile. It was, perhaps, in return for this timely loan that, upon the spoliation of the churches, the Opéra was presented with a chime of bells, unfortunately destroyed in the fire of 1873. M. Nuitter mentions a tradition, impossible to verify, that one of these bells came from the Church of St. Germain l'Auxerrois, and after having been used to give the signal for the real massacre of St. Bartholomew, it had again tolled the alarm during the five hundred performances of Meyerbeer's "Huguenots."

But the downfall of the monarchy and the subsequent anarchy had its influence on the box-office of the National Academy of Music as well as on its stage. Like everything else, the Opéra felt the beneficent effect of paper money issued by the people for the people. With the unlimited putting forth of assignats, the price of tickets was rapidly raised, until a seat in the boxes cost 9,000 livres. The 18th Prairial, Year IV., the receipts of the Opéra were 1,071,350 livres! The real value of this million of livres was a little over two hundred dollars.

Under the Empire and the Restoration the Opéra prospered. In 1822 it spent 188,260 francs upon the mounting of one piece, "Aladdin, or the Marvellous Lamp." In February, 1820, as the Duke of Berri was handing his wife into her carriage, he was assassinated. In consequence, the Government razed the building and gave the ground to the public as the Place Louvois. A temporary home was found for the National Academy of Music in the Rue Lepeletier, and there it remained for more than fifty years, until the night of October 28, 1873, when the building caught fire. Within a few hours it was burnt to the ground. As M. de la Salle, the author of an ample and amusing history of "Les Treize Salles de l'Opéra," walked home from the fire, he saw by the early dawn the wet and just posted bill of the Opéra announcing the "one-hundredth performance of 'Hamlet' for this evening at 7 1-2 o'clock."

The half century which the National Academy of

The Academy of Music.

Music passed in the theatre built for it in the Rue Lepeletier was the most glorious period of its existence. The French people are very proud of their chief musical theatre, and it is in the history of these fifty-two years—from August, 1821, when the opera-house, on which work had been begun as soon as the Duke of Berri died, was first thrown open to the public, to the dismal day in October, 1873, when it was wholly destroyed by fire—it is in the history of these years that there is most to be proud of. The house proved to have remarkable acoustic qualities, and it was the first of all the Parisian playhouses to be lighted by gas. To these physical advantages an artistic superiority over almost every other musical theatre in Europe was soon added.

For two score of years the history of the French Academy of Music—by turns Royal, National, and Imperial—was in a great measure the history of opera itself. Half of the operas composed during this period, and retaining the stage to-day, were written especially for the Paris Opéra. After Lulli, Rameau, Glück, Sacchini, and Spontini, who had rendered its stage illustrious in the past, there soon came forward Rossini and Meyerbeer, who were to make it even more famous in the present. But a little behind these two great musicians came Auber and Halévy, who gave to the Opéra some of their best work.

As may be seen by a glance down this list of names, the French Academy of Music has always been hospitable to foreigners. Owing its solid foundation to an Italian, Lulli, it has extended an open welcome to the German Glück and Meyerbeer, as well as to the Italian Piccini, Spontini, and Rossini, while at the same time offering a broad stage to the native Rameau, Grétry, Halévy, and Auber. It was perhaps to this very cosmopolitanism, this freedom from the narrowness of nationality, which only too often tends to degenerate into the groove of petty provincialism, that the Opéra owed its broad and vigorous vitality. The Paris Opéra built itself up by attracting to it the rising musical geniuses of Europe, be they French, or Italian, or German, and by attaching them to it by liberal treatment. The capital of France is one of the cities of the world in which the foreigner, in the end, feels most at home. Rossini and Meyerbeer became pure Parisians, in spite of their accident of birth.

And herein the Paris of our time is wiser than the Rome of old; invaded alike by the barbarians attracted by their riches and promise, Paris has been able to assimilate matter which in Rome remained barbarian to the end. Paris not only drew to itself and made like unto itself the outsider, but it made the best of him. Nowhere is this fact more obvious than in the history of the French musical drama.

It is not too much to say that by far the larger part of the fame of the Opéra is due to the works there produced by foreigners. In the very half century now to be considered, the French Halévy and Auber did not shed so much lustre on its stage as the German Meyerbeer or the Italian Rossini. Of course the credit of the success is still due to the French themselves; the great foreigners would not have come to France if it had not been made worth their while. The pecuniary inducements were considerable, but it may be doubted whether the artistic temptations were not even more powerful. The composer could be sure that there would be no stinted attempt to realize his ideal; he could rely on lavish and elaborate mounting and scenery; he could count on all the resources of a musical organization second to none then in existence; he could certainly have at his call a picked company of singers trained in the best schools and unusually strong in dramatic ability; and above all, and perhaps more important than the other considerations in the eyes of a composer seeking to do work which might survive him, he could confidently expect a good libretto.

The French are a nation of playwrights, and in no department of dramatic literature is their skill more evident than in the making of opera books. And how important the book is, no one who has ever read the biography of a composer needs to be told. A bad libretto has killed more than one score which otherwise might have had a fair chance of life; and even where its defects have not been fatal; even where, as in the case of the "Magic Flute," the exceeding beauty and strength of the music has been strong enough to bear up beneath the exceeding feebleness and folly of the book, the struggle has been a hard one. In all its history the Opéra has been fortunate in its librettos, from the early days of Quinault and the younger Corneille to the comparatively recent productions of Scribe. Of course a poor libretto has caused the failure of good music at the Opéra as well as elsewhere, but the average of success has been surprisingly high.

It must not be supposed that even the successful books were all of them wholly exempt from the peculiarities, not to say impossibilities, which are only too frequent in librettos; they had their full share of absurdities, but they answered their purpose. Scribe's librettos, for example, are models of what an opera book should be. Dramatic in plot, fertile in situation, lending themselves readily to scenic display, providing for the proper introduction of choruses and processions, telling a story simple in itself and capable of being shown almost wholly in action, cut—to use the French phrase—so as to show the musician to best advantage, they are admirably adapted to the end in view. Scribe's collaborators and competitors, having so fine a model before their eyes, did work nearly as good. In considering the use of the modern grand opera, the services of Scribe are not to be passed over slightingly. It is to his influence, in a measure at least, and to his keen eye for the capabilities of the modern stage, that we owe the pre-Wagnerian opera; and it may be questioned whether—if taking Wagner as a writer of opera books merely—whether he did not begin where Scribe left off. All the mechanical marvels which were exhibited to the throng of worshippers which gathered in the theatre at Bayreuth were but the development of suggestions to be seen in the librettos of Scribe.

When the Academy of Music, in 1821, moved into the new opera-house in the Rue Lepeletier, its musical organization was far from perfect. It was deficient in singers, and for some time its great reliance had been on the ballet. Under the enervating influence of the Empire, French music had wellnigh fallen into a state of nullity. So low was it that two composers were coupled to set one weak libretto; at times even three collaborated. In 1821, for instance, Cherubini was linked with Berton in making the music of a now forgotten "Blanche de Provence;" and in 1825 Berton, Kreutzer, and Boïeldieu joined together to compose an equally dead and gone "Pharamond." But in 1824, Rossini, fresh from the successes won in Italy with the

"Barber of Seville," "Othello," and "Semiramis," arrived in Paris from London, where he had just made £7,000 in five months. Appointed general inspector of singing at the Academy of Music, he first strengthened the company of vocalists and then taught them how to sing as he wished them. A year later he brought out his first French opera, the "Siege of Corinth," much of the music of which had already served him in Italy in a "Mahomet."

He made two other similar rearrangements of his pre-existing music, and then, on the 3d of August, 1829, he brought out the first grand opera, which he had written expressly for the Opéra, and which must be considered as the first grand opera of a new school, neither Italian nor German, but to be called French, for want of a better name. This opera was "William Tell." After making this masterpiece Rossini laid down his pen; either he felt that he could not surpass it, or, having once shown what he was capable of, his natural and national laziness seized on him, so that he had no desire to make another attempt. Be the reason what it may, the first grand opera written by Rossini in French remained the last he wrote at all.

M. Alphonse Royer, the author of the libretto of the "Favorite," and for a time the manager of the Academy of Music, in a history of the Opéra which he published in 1875, suggested that the revolution of 1830 was the indirect cause of Rossini's retirement. Louis Philippe was a saving and economical king. As soon as he was firmly on the throne he reformed his civil list. The Opéra as a royal institution had been closely connected with the royal household, and, relying on the royal purse, an agreement had been made with Rossini, whereby, in consideration of an annuity of six thousand francs and a premium of fifteen thousand more on the delivery of each score, the composer was to bring out five new operas in the next ten years. The new officials refused to recognize this annuity. As M. Royer sharply puts it, " they went to law for five years to economize the six thousand francs, and not to have Rossini's five new operas. In the end they did not have them—a great triumph! But they had to pay the pension!"

Another reason for Rossini's seemingly premature withdrawal is also given by M. Royer. It was the grand chorus of admiration which had greeted the production of " Robert the Devil." Rossini could not brook a brother near the throne, not even one whose early steps he himself had guided. It was Rossini, the manager of the Italian theatre, who had brought out three of Meyerbeer's earliest operas. " Robert the Devil " was originally a comic opera—that is to say, the dialogue was spoken, and there were no recitatives—but seeing a chance at the Opéra, Scribe and Delavigne hastily rhymed their prose, and Meyerbeer improvised the needed music; and on the 21st of November, 1831, "Robert the Devil" took Paris by storm. In February, 1836, came the "Huguenots;" and thirteen years later, in April, 1849, the "Prophet" followed. These were the only three grand operas written for the Opéra which Meyerbeer lived to see acted. A fourth, the "Africaine," was brought out in April, 1865, after his death.

While Rossini and Meyerbeer are the two greatest names of the past seventy-five years in the history of the Opéra, they are not the only great names. In 1828 was first produced the "Muette de Portici," known to us as "Masaniello," and recognized everywhere as one of the best and brightest of Auber's works. Another Frenchman, Halévy, not long after composed the "Jewess," the one opera by which he is known to opera-goers outside of Paris. In 1840 Donizetti saw his "Favorite" produced at the Opéra, with a success which endures to this day. Among the singers whose efforts aided in putting the Opéra in the front rank of all European opera-houses, and whose skill and natural gifts were at the command of the composers I have named, were Adolph Nourrit, Levasseur, Mme. Cinti-Damoreau, Mme. Falcon, Mme. Stolz, Mme. Alboni, Duprez, and Roger. In the ballet were Marie Taglioni, Fanny Elssler, and Carlotta Grisi.

In later days these great singers have been followed by others better known to contemporary opera-goers—M. Faure, Mme. Sasse, Mme. Nilsson, Mme. Adelina Patti, Mme. Carvalho. And the more recent operas—at least those of them which have been successful, the fate of barely a third of those produced—are equally familiar in the ears of all. In 1861 an adaptation of Herr Wagner's "Tannhäuser" was brought out. M. Royer notes that the first performance took place on a thirteenth—the thirteenth of March. Perhaps the unlucky date was the cause of its summary damning; perhaps its untimely taking off was due to the organized hostility of the Jockey Club, disgusted that there was no ballet in the middle of the opera as was the custom; perhaps there was some other equally potent influence at work against the ill-starred opera—at all events, after three performances, all alike stormy and tumultuous, it was withdrawn.

Evidence is not now wanting that the more cool and collected portion of the French public is beginning to regret the violence exhibited when the opera was produced. In the exhaustive catalogue of the library of the Opéra prepared by M. Lajarte, the musical librarian, only completed in 1878, a chronological list is given of all the musical works produced or performed at the Academy of Music, and from the note appended to the "Tannhäuser" it seems that the extreme distaste for the Teutonic music is disappearing. "We ought to confess," says M. Lajarte, "that his score contains beauties of the first rank in the midst of ridiculous inanities. The summary justice inflicted on it by the Parisian public is, consequently, a fault we shall not try to excuse."

From the seventh part of this invaluable catalogue, covering the time from the first performance of the "Prophet," in 1849, to the middle of 1876, many interesting details may be gleaned. In it we are reminded that M. Emile Augier once wrote an opera libretto, "Sappho," for which M. Gounod composed the music, and it was a failure; we note that M. Offenbach, in 1860, wrote the music of a ballet, the "Butterfly," for which the celebrated dancer, Marie Taglioni, composed the dancing, and it too was a failure. Apropos of ballets, it is with some surprise that the name of Théophile Gautier is seen so often as the author of ballet librettos; his beautiful "Giselle," for which Adolphe Adam composed the music, is an excellent example of the skill with which, catching at a suggestion of Hoffmann's, he could put a fanciful and fantastic subject on the stage. Among the opera librettists the name of M. Got, the great comedian of the Comédie Française, is twice to be found.

Besides these merely curious gleanings, we are told of the more important and longer-lived works which the Opéra has of late years produced. It was for the Academy of Music that M. Ambroise

The Academy of Music. 37

Thomas wrote his "Hamlet," acted with most extraordinary effect by M. Faure and Mme. Nilsson. It was to the Academy that M. Gounod saw his "Faust" transferred after it had made its mark at the now no longer existing Théâtre Lyrique. It was for the Academy of Music that Signor Verdi, in 1867, wrote his "Don Carlos." It was at the Academy of Music that the lovely ballet of oriental fantasy, the "Source," of M. Leo Délibes, danced into fame and fortune. And with this list closes the account of the half century which the Opéra spent in the Rue Lepeletier. With the burning of that theatre in 1873, and the transfer of the Academy of Music (after an interval) to the new and unequalled theatre which M. Garnier had erected for it, begins another chapter of its history, too few of the annual pages of which have as yet turned for us to be able to prognosticate with any degree of accuracy the final result.

But before taking leave of the opera-house in the Rue Lepeletier, mention must be made of one of the most extraordinary coincidences in history. On the evening of January 14th, 1858, was given the farewell benefit performance of a singer named Massol. The programme consisted of fragments of "Masaniello," in which there is a revolt against a viceroy; of three acts of "Maria Stuarda," performed by Signora Ristori, and in this play a sovereign is executed; and of the second act of "William

Tell," in which there is again a conspiracy against royal authority. While this revolutionary programme was about to be gone through on the stage of the Opéra, preparations were making for a still more bloody attack on the monarch of France. As the Emperor and Empress turned into the Rue Lepeletier the murderous bombs of Orsini exploded, sparing the imperial target, but maiming many an innocent man accidentally present.

CHAPTER III.

THE NEW OPÉRA.

It is now a little over five years since the new Opéra was completed; it is not yet twenty since it was definitely decided upon. Toward the end of 1860 an imperial decree announced that a competition would be opened for plans for the new building. Although only a month was allowed for preparation, one hundred and seventy-one plans were submitted. The authors of the five best designs competed again amongst themselves, and as a final result M. Charles Garnier was chosen as the architect. Like most Frenchmen, M. Garnier is nothing if not logical. His views of what a theatre ought to be are set forth with logical exactness in an interesting book of his called the "Théâtre."

Unlike most men who have laid down the law, M. Garnier was enabled to carry out his ideas on a grand scale. The successive steps, from the tearing down of block after block of old houses, and the opening of street after street, to the final crowning of the completed edifice, are all to be found recorded in a little book on the "Nouvel Opéra," dedicated to M. Garnier, and written by M. Charles Nuitter, the archivist of the institution. From this volume the facts in the few following pages are for the most part borrowed. Three of the full-page wood-cuts which adorned M. Nuitter's text are reproduced here to illustrate these brief abstracts from it.

Owing to the exceptional depth required beneath the stage, twenty metres (nearly sixty-five feet), great delay was experienced in the work from the bursting of the springs, of which the soil was full. It took a year's hard work to pump out the water, and when the foundations were laid they had to be protected by very massive walls, and by a series of reversed arches so arranged that external pressure would only consolidate the work more firmly. In July, 1862, Count Walewski laid the corner-stone, and by the end of the year the foundations were finished. In 1864 the side walls were fully up, and the next year the wings were partly covered in. Money falling short, work was suspended on the interior to finish the exterior, and on the Bonapartist holiday of the Exhibition year, August 15th, 1867, the enormous scaffolding, filled with innumerable glass sashes, which concealed the front of the building, was knocked away and fell forward, revealing the head and front of M. Garnier's design. Two years later the roof was completed. And then came the war with Prussia, followed at once by civil strife in the streets of Paris. All work on the building ceased. It was used at first as a hospital, and then as a storehouse. The weights imposed on its floors and arches sometimes made the architect tremble, but the excellent workmanship resisted every strain.

During the siege of Paris a detachment of sailors used the roof as a signal station to communicate with the outlying forts. During the rule of the Commune, the same station served the improvised authorities to send off the fire balloons which they had loaded with incendiary proclamations to the people of France. When the national government regained possession of the capital, it was found that perhaps three hundred thousand francs would repair all the damage done. Work was resumed at once, in spite of diminished appropriations. The day after the fire which destroyed the theatre in the Rue Lepeletier, M. Garnier, on his personal credit, pushed everything to the utmost possible speed. In a few months ample appropriations were made, and by the end of 1874 the building was handed over to the manager of the Opéra.

No detailed description of the front of the building, nor of the main architectural features, is needed; the engraving which serves as a frontispiece to this volume speaks for itself. M. Garnier holds that there are three parts of a theatre—the entrance hall, the auditorium, and the stage. Believing not only that construction should not be hidden, but that it should be obvious, he has placed first the low-lying division of the building, which contains the entrances, exits, waiting-rooms, and the famous staircase. Rising roundly above this is the circular dome of the auditorium. Sharply towering behind this, again, is the abrupt roof of the stage. Each of the three divisions is distinct, and a lateral view shows at once the intention of each.

Entering the Opéra either in the centre, if you come on foot, or at the side, if you roll up in your carriage, you arrive at once in the grand circular vestibule under the auditorium. From this a few steps bring you out on the grand staircase, upon which, or rather upon the galleries which frame it, each tier of the theatre opens. By means of this staircase and these galleries the spectators reach their boxes or seats before the opera begins, and also between its acts go from them to the grand *foyer*. Unpleasant as it is to be forced to use a French word, there is really in this case no exact equivalent in English; the *foyer* is the apartment, large or small as may be, which in every French theatre is used as a promenade between the acts. We have not the word, perhaps because we have not the thing. French theatres in general are so badly ventilated, and soon become so unendurably hot, and the waits between the acts are so much longer than is usual with us, that a necessity exists for some airy hall in which we may stretch our legs

THE GRAND STAIRCASE.

cramped by close quarters. The *foyer* of the Opéra, like that of the Théâtre Français, is a sight to be seen for its own sake, even if there were no physical need of it.

The *foyer*—since the word must be used—extends across the front of the building. It is fifty-four metres long, thirteen wide, and eighteen high. (Elderly readers may like to be reminded that a metre is about a yard and a tenth.) The design of the staircase and the decoration of this *foyer* may be considered M. Garnier's chief claims to future fame as a great artist. In both he has rioted in richness of color. M. Nuitter tells us that M. Garnier has been called the Veronese of architects, and that more than once M. Garnier has accosted him with a brief " I am going away to-night."

" Where ? " the surprised archivist would ask.

" To Italy," would reply the architect ; " I begin to feel myself attacked by the white and gold of the restaurants, and I am going off there to look for a little color."

And off he would go for a week, rushing away to the Pitti Palace, and returning full of new vigor and fresh suggestions.

On the ceiling of this *foyer* are the celebrated paintings of M. Paul Baudry. There are two grand allegorical compositions on the sides of a central picture representing the union of Melody and Harmony, between Poetry and Glory. Two secondary paintings show Comedy and Tragedy. Ten large compositions show the effects of music and the dance, and the triumphs of beauty. The intervals between these are occupied by single figures of eight of the muses—Philosophy having been left without a representative. Over the doors are oval panels in which children are depicted with instruments symbolic of the music of various countries. This rapid enumeration may serve to show the extent of M. Paul Baudry's artistic labors; their beauties I have neither space nor qualifications adequately to portray. It may suffice to say that when first exhibited to the art-lovers of Paris, they were at once recognized as among the finest works of French pictorial genius of this century. It is with general regret that we are told of the deterioration they are now undergoing from the effects of the gas used to illuminate the *foyer*. Either one of the new electric lights must be substituted for the present noxious gas, or the paintings must be removed and copies substituted. M. Garnier has as yet found no electric lamp satisfactory as a light for pictures. He hopes to be able to replace M. Baudry's original paintings with copies of them made in mosaic. One of the ten oval panels over the doors of the *foyer* is already in mosaic; perhaps before the gas does any great damage, M. Garnier's ever-active ingenuity may devise some economical method of reproducing the rest of them in the same material.

THE GRAND FOYER

At each end of the main *foyer* is an octagonal hall, prolonging the perspective. The ceilings of these are in like manner decorated with oil paintings—in this case by M. Delaunay and M. Barrias. This is but a hasty description of the *foyer* and its appendages; to describe it adequately, as M. Nuitter says, would take a volume.

In front of the *foyer*, between it and the external air, is the *loggia*, an open gallery, overlooking the approaches to the Opéra, and giving a long view down the Avenue de l'Opéra to the Théâtre Français. Easy access is had to the *loggia* from the *foyer* by double glass doors, so that no draft penetrates into the interior. No sharper contrast could well be imagined than to turn from the church scene of the "Prophet," or the prison scene of "Faust," and to stand in the outer air gazing down on the bustle and hurry of nocturnal life along the crossing streets and boulevards of modern Paris.

Before going inside the building again, mention should be made of the many statues in bronze and in marble which adorn the outside. As a glance at the engraving of the façade will show, M. Garnier believes that sculpture is the handmaiden of architecture, and he has put a statue wherever he could. Up on the attic front are two bronze groups by M. Guméry, representing Harmony and Poetry. At the main entrance are four groups in marble, devoted to Music, Lyric Poetry, Lyric

Drama, and the Dance. This last was the work of the late M. Carpeaux, who delighted in Bernini-like effects. When his group was first shown it excited a bitter polemic. It was denounced as indecent by some, and defended as innocent by others. Articles and pamphlets pro and con came forth in rapid succession. At length one of the assailants, tired perhaps of wasting his ink uselessly in a paper war, broke a bottle of it over the statue. Fortunately the stains were readily obliterated. Possibly to take away all temptation to a repetition of the offence, the authorities removed the rather excited figures of M. Carpeaux to the interior of the building, and a more chaste group by M. Guméry was ordered for the exterior.

Returning again to the interior of the house, and passing up the monumental staircase, and along a corridor, we come into the auditorium. The first impression is that it is too small—far too small. But this is only an impression; it is not a fact. The false impression is caused by the altogether abnormal grandeur of the approaches. The size of the staircase, for instance, is such as to make one expect to find a theatre of full twice the size of that which one enters. The exact fact is that the auditorium of the Opéra is among the largest in the world. In seating capacity it is but little the inferior of any opera-house, as may be seen by this little table of the number of places in each of the chief operatic theatres of the world:

Fenice, Venice	2,000 seats.
Academy of Music, New York.	2,000 "
Carlo Felice, Genoa..........	2,000 "
San Carlos, Lisbon...........	2,000 "
Opéra, Paris	2,100 "
Royal Theatre, Munich.......	2,300 "
Opera, Vienna...............	2,400 "
Covent Garden, London......	2,500 "
La Scala, Milan	3,000 "

In the old opera-house in the Rue Lepeletier there were places for only 1,783 persons.

If, however, the auditorium is not remarkable for its great size, the stage is. M. Nuitter declares that it is the largest in the world. Its depth is not phenomenal, but in width and height it surpasses all its rivals. In case special depth should be required, a long passage behind the stage, some six metres wide, can be thrown open to the eye of the spectator; and behind this again is the magnificent green-room of the ballet, which can also be utilized if need be—thus giving a total depth of nearly fifty metres. The stage is not only the finest in extent, it is also the most elaborately equipped with machinery of all kinds. All the supports of the stage, all the devices for lowering and hoisting the scenes, all the beams which sustain the traps, all the manifold frameworks needed for the proper presentation of richly spectacular operas and ballets, are not in wood, as in other theatres, but in iron, thus lessening the number and reducing the size of the forest of posts and beams which always seem to hold up the stage in other theatres.

The mention, a few lines ago, of the magnificent green-room of the ballet brings me naturally to the consideration of a remarkable peculiarity of the Opéra. In the early days of the modern theatre spectators were freely allowed on the stage; they stood and sat and encumbered the boards to such an extent that when Voltaire brought out his tragedy of "Semiramis" (for which he had borrowed some of the effects of the "Hamlet" he had reviled), the ghost could not come forward until the ushers had besought space for him, crying "Room, gentlemen, room if you please for monsieur the ghost!" It was perhaps this perilling of tragic dignity which led to the abating of the nuisance. At all events, in the last century a reform was made, and no spectators were allowed anywhere behind the curtain either of the Opéra or of the two great theatres, the French and Italian Comedies. One exception, however, was made at the Opéra, an exception which rules to this day.

The regular subscribers, taking their seats three nights a week during the season, have the right of admission to the green-room of the ballet. This custom, as to the morality of which it may be as well to say nothing, has obtained since 1770, when the Opéra took possession of its house in the Palais Royal. In 1774 a royal edict forbade all communication between the public and the performers, but it soon fell into abeyance. In the new house of M. Garnier, the right of certain privileged persons to come into the green-room of the ballet is frankly acknowledged, and due preparation in consequence is made for their reception. The green-room of the ballet is a magnificent hall a little behind the stage, decorated almost as extravagantly as the *foyer* in the front of the house. Portraits of the great ballet-dancers who have succeeded one another on the stage of the Opéra, and of the great ballet-composers, fill panels on the walls; and on the ceiling are four grand panels by M. Boulanger, representing the War Dance, the Country Dance, the Love Dance, and the Bacchic Dance. It is in this green-room that the day rehearsals of the ballet are held; and here at night come the dancers to try a step or two before appearing in front of the footlights. To facilitate practice, the floor slopes just like that of the stage. Iron bars covered with velvet are affixed to all the walls for the dancers to lay hold of while indulging in the preliminary exercises which serve to loosen the joints and make them supple.

It is difficult to overestimate the important position which the ballet holds at the Academy of Music. We, in America, scarcely know what a good ballet is. Fine dancers we have had in plenty. The chief dancer to-day at the Opéra is the Mlle. Rita Sangalli who made her first great success in New York in the "Black Crook," now fourteen years ago. But the ballets we have seen have been incidental ballets; and beyond two or three star dancers the quality was mediocre. Now the beauty of a ballet lies in the merit of all the dancers, in the uniformity of drill and harmony of execution evident in all from the highest to the lowest.

This of course we cannot have, or hope to have, in America as long as the ballet is a mere itinerant accident. A good three-act ballet pantomime, like the "Source" of M. Leo Delibes, or the "Yedda" of M. Olivier Métra, telling a simple but dramatic story in three well contrasted acts, would be little less than a revelation in New York. In Paris the ballet is not an incident; it is an institution. An engagement there is a settlement for life. It robs the cradle and the grave. It trains the young and it pensions the old. Man may be found there in each of his seven ages, and woman in her solitary one. One of the leading dancing-masters of Paris, M. l'Enfant, told me that he had been in the ballet of the Opéra for fifty-four years; he had gone on at six as a Cupid, passing slowly through the grades of tiny imp, young lover, and heavy villain, to the dignity of noble father; he had retired on a pension at the age of sixty, thereafter amusing his leisure, and increasing his income, by arranging the germans of the Faubourg St. Germain.

In the beginning of the second quarter of this century, when the ruler of the Opéra was Dr. Véron, from whose garrulous memoirs many curious items can be gathered of the secrets of his management, and of his trials and tribulations at the hands of a bevy of beauties over whom he ruled, there appeared upon the boards in rapid succession a galaxy of dancing stars whose like has never been seen before or since. Paul, Albert, Perrot, among the men; Taglioni, Elssler, Cerito, Grisi, Duvernay, among the women, were a few of the leading lights. As the ballet-masters he had Taglioni, the father of his daughter, and Vestris, the son and grandson of his ancestors. Dr. Véron spared no expense in mounting a ballet like the "Sylphide," or an opera like "Robert the Devil," with the weird dance in which Mademoiselle Taglioni appears as the Abbess. It was the period of the greatest prosperity that the ballet has ever known. And its power in the Opéra of Paris has never been broken since. Nowhere is it more potent. Whatever may be the opera which divides the bill with the ballet—even though it be the "Orpheus" of Glück—matters little; it is not heard. "On n'entend que le ballet," as the saying goes; "They only listen to the ballet." To the might of the Parisian adorers of Terpsichore is due the damning of Herr Wagner's " Tannhäuser "—at least so it has been said.

To keep up this training school for dancers, to support the daily expense of an institution so gigantic as the Opéra, to meet the pay-roll of sometimes five hundred names, to satisfy the exorbitant demands of star singers, to mount every opera with the utmost sumptuousness, to be prepared for the multifarious requisitions which may at any time be made, is no easy task for one man, and no private purse is equal to it. The Opéra has rarely been able to pay its annual expenses, and the government has to come to the rescue. The subvention has varied from three hundred thousand a year during the first Republic to nine hundred and fifty thousand under the Restoration. The present subvention is midway between these extremes. This yearly contribution of the nation to the cause of musical and Terpsichorean art is in addition to the use rent free of the building itself, erected at a cost of not far from fifty millions of francs (say ten millions of dollars), the annual interest on which at three *per cent.*, the current rate in France for government loans, is three hundred thousand dollars. In one way or another it may be said that the support of the Opéra in Paris costs the people of France very nearly half a million of dollars a year.

The New Opéra.

The advocates of the paternal theory of government will be pleased to learn that when the building was in progress a state commission was appointed to discuss the best method of scene-shifting. And the civil service reformers may be glad to be told that the vacancies in the orchestra are always filled by competitive examination.

It is with the view of making up for any possible loss that, during each winter, a certain number of masked balls are given at the Opéra. By means of devices invented originally by a monk, the auditorium and the stage can be floored over in a few hours. There are generally four balls, of which the best is the one nearest to Ash-Wednesday. Two bands, led by the first bandmasters of Paris, provide the music, various special waltzes being nearly always written for the occasion. But it is not necessary to dilate on the opera balls. Everybody has heard of them. It may be noted, however, that at the first ball given in the new Opéra, American soda-water—"d'excellents sodas glacés à l'Américaine," so a gossiper of the *Figaro* called them—were among the favorite beverages; this shows rapid progress on the part of the Parisians, for it was only nine years since they had their first taste of this delectable beverage at the American restaurant in the Exhibition of 1867.

High up in the top of one of the side semicircular pavilions of the Opéra, six or seven stories above the level of the surrounding streets, are the ample apartments set aside for the archives and the library. After the daring visitor has entered the stage door and mounted the seemingly interminable steps, he comes out into long corridors lined with presses, in which are stored the many precious musical MSS. of the Opéra acquired during its two hundred years of existence; in glazed cases on the top of these presses are exposed certain of the more curious autographs. The musical MSS., and all the music, in fact, printed or engraved, are under the care of M. Théodore de Lajarte, the musical librarian, and he it is who has prepared the "Catalogue de la Bibliothèque Musicale du Théâtre de l'Opéra," already referred to. In the second volume of this invaluable work is an etching, by M. Le Rat, of the ample oval room at the top of the pavilion, in which is now ranged the dramatic, operatic, Terpsichorean, and generally theatrical library of the Opéra, under the care of M. Nuitter, the archivist. This collection is, perhaps, the best theatrical library in Paris, and it is rapidly growing. Both English and German drama and dramatic biography are well represented in it, and it is altogether more cosmopolitan than French collections usually are. M. Nuitter himself is my authority for saying that, as soon as he has filled a few more vacancies, he proposes issuing a catalogue, which will certainly be one of the most important in its class. In time he hopes to be able to move his precious collections from their present lofty elevation to more accessible quarters on the lower floor of what was designed as the imperial pavilion. The Bonaparte family having no immediate use for it, no better destination could be suggested than this. An attempt has been made to secure for the Opéra what is left of the unequalled collection of theatrical books and pamphlets made by the late Baron Taylor.

Before leaving the Opéra finally, it may be of interest to some readers interested in musical history to draw up from the latest issues of the "Almanach des Spectacles" a statement of the comparative popularity of the chief works of the French school. Up to the beginning of last year—

Meyerbeer's	"Robert the Devil"	had been given	632 times.
"	"Huguenots"	"	"	656	"
"	"Prophet"	"	"	382	"
"	"Africaine"	"	"	281	"
Rossini's	"William Tell"	"	"	632	"
Donizetti's	"Favorite"	"	"	499	"
M. Gounod's	"Faust"	"	"	279	"
M. Thomas's	"Hamlet"	"	"	156	"
Halévy's	"Jewess"	"	"	436	"
Mozart's	"Don Juan"	"	"	174	"

Of these ten operas "Faust" is the only one which was not written for the Opéra and originally produced there. A record like this is one of which any theatre might well be proud.

CHAPTER IV.

THE OTHER MUSICAL THEATRES.

THE Italian opera of Paris no longer exists, and the owners of the youthful and feminine hearts which have thrilled at the touching strains of Owen Meredith's "Aux Italiens" may now be reminded that it is not now possible to be "at the Italiens," for the simple reason that the Salle Ventadour, sacred to the music of the south, has been sold to a banking company, and turned into offices from which issue notes of a more substantial value than those emitted from the throats of Mme. Patti and M. Nicolini. Having no longer any home in Paris, Italian opera has only visited it of late sparingly. And even before the alienation of the Salle Ventadour, which took place early in 1879, for several years the success of Italian opera in Paris had been doubtful. Unlike the English and Americans, the French like opera in their own tongue, and while in both London and New York the Italian opera-house holds the foremost position among the musical theatres of the city, both artistically and fashionably, in Paris it does not. There the Opéra is at once the resort of the best society and the headquarters of musicians. Second to the Opéra, and coming before the Italian theatre, even when it was in the height of its glory, is the Opéra Comique. (Some non-musical readers may need to be reminded that a "comic opera" is not necessarily comic; it is so called to distinguish it from "grand opera.")

In Paris comic opera is indigenous, and Italian opera is an exotic, and, without external aid, it languishes there as it does here. Its success in Paris, as in America, has been spasmodic, depending rather upon the excitement created by one star, than the harmony of the whole. Now, although the Opéra and Opéra Comique have had many great singers, their strength has always lain not in the exceptional superiority of an individual, but in the general excellence of the whole. The style in which pieces are put upon the stage was no better in the Salle Ventadour that it is in our Academy; there was the same polyglot company with half-Italianized names, the same absurd scenery and costumes, the same lack of care and taste and style. In Paris Italian opera flourished only in the hot-bed of fashion, and but for a season; it bloomed but to wither, and in most respects its history there is very like its history here. Many of the operas which we are accustomed to hear in Italian, in New York, were originally written in French for the Opéra or for the Opéra Comique, and are constantly performed at one theatre or the other. The manager of the Salle Ventadour had therefore to rely either on the early and well-worn operas of the few first-rate Italian composers, who had not written specially for the Paris public, or on the latest novelties, which are always ticklish commodities, not having yet received the stamp of popular approval. The final efforts to attract paying audiences to the house were made by a music publisher, who brought out Signor Verdi's "Aïda," and by M. Capoul, who wanted to appear as *Romeo* in the Marquis d'Ivry's "Lovers of Verona," and so took the theatre to attempt the part. And this last play, it is to be noted, was given in French. A few weeks after *Romeo* had sung his dying song, the Salle Ventadour was handed over to the carpenters and masons, and Paris had one theatre the less.

In one peculiarity, at least, Italian opera in Paris differed from the same amusement in New York. In both cities it occupied for specified seasons a house erected especially for it, and in both reliance must be had more or less on subscriptions made in advance for the whole number of specified performances. Now in New York the subscriber pays for his box and takes his tickets, and there is no further demand on his purse. But in Paris the payment for the tickets only secured to him the right of admission; he had in addition to pay for carpeting the box, and for furnishing it, and for lighting it, and for heating it.

The Opéra Comique is one of the oldest theatres in Paris. It is the outgrowth of the strolling companies of comedians who pitched their tents at the fairs in the environs of Paris in the early part of the last century. The royal and privileged theatres sought to prevent this suburban rivalry, and royal edicts from time to time fell with heavy force on the sprightly and often personal performances of the travelling bands. At one period the actors of the fair were forbidden to sing or speak. The ingenuity of French dramatists, chief among whom was Le Sage, the author of "Gil Blas," devised means of overcoming this prohibition. The story of the play was told in pantomime until words were wanted, and then the actor took from his pocket a huge scroll, on which, when unrolled, the spectators could read the required phrase. The prohibition as to speech was thus evaded; and the method of getting around that against singing was equally ingenious. At the appropriate moment a placard descended from the folds of the drop-curtain, having on it the words of the song, and an indication of the popular tune to which they could be sung, seeing which, and knowing that the actors were debarred from executing it, the audience would very kindly sing the stanza themselves.

In 1762 the chief actors of the fair companies joined one of the three privileged theatres—the Italian Comedy, the successors of the comedians who had shared on alternate nights Molière's stage. The language of the theatre became French, with an occasional dropping into Italian. In 1780, all but one of the surviving Italian actors went back to Italy; but the company still continued to be successful, and to bear the title of the Italian Comedy. In 1792, at the height of the growing patriotic feeling of that time, the name was changed to National Opéra Comique. All through the Revolution, and the Republic, and the Empire, and the Restoration, and coming in of the Orleans branch, and the second Republic, and the second Empire, and the third Republic, in good days and in evil days, the Opéra Comique was prosperous. It is only of late that its popularity seems to have somewhat waned. It receives an annual subvention from the government, which keeps up its staff, and pays its pensions, and gives a solidity to the institution for the most part lacking in merely private enterprises.

Among the operas which the Opéra Comique has given to the world are some of the best works of Grétry, Auber, Boiëldieu, M. Ambroise Thomas, and M. Charles Gounod. A long list might be made of pieces which every opera-goer would recognize at sight, although they have more often been heard in this country in Italian or English than in French. Mention must be made of Auber's "Crown Diamonds," and "Fra Diavolo," of

Meyerbeer's "Star of the North," of Hérold's "Zampa," of Bizet's "Carmen," and of M. Ambroise Thomas's "Mignon." In these two last operas the chief parts, so strongly contrasted, were both created—to use the French phrase—by Mme. Galli-Marié, the elder sister of the Mme. Irma-Marié who was one of the earliest expounders of opéra bouffe in these United States, and also of Mme. Paola-Marié, one of the latest. M. Capoul, M. Achard, and Mme. Marie Cabel have also at different times held leading positions at the Opéra Comique, which, however, like its big brother the Opéra, relies rather on the whole than the part, rather on the smoothness of an entire performance than the merit of a single star.

At various times the need has been felt of a third French opera-house—the Italian opera not being considered—which should play musical dramas not light enough for the Opéra Comique, and not important or elaborate enough for the Opéra. To supply this want, and to give young composers a chance to produce themselves, the city built the Théâtre Lyrique in the Place du Châtelet. Under the direction of M. Carvalho, in the years before the troubles of 1870, the Théâtre Lyrique had a prosperous career. It transferred works from the German and Italian—although but sparingly—and it brought out new French operas. The "Rienzi" of Herr Wagner, and the "Faust," "Mireille," and "Romeo and Juliet," of M. Gounod were first heard within its walls; since then M. Gounod's masterpiece has been adopted by the Opéra, whither Mme. Miolan Carvalho, the wife of the manager, and the original *Marguerite*, has also gone to sing it.

During the Commune the Théâtre Lyrique was burnt. When it was finally rebuilt the title and the subvention had gone to the Théâtre de la Gaité, where M. Vizentini endeavored to repeat M. Carvalho's success. But he had good luck only with M. Victor Massé's " Paul and Virginia," and after struggling vainly with the unending expense of unremunerative operatic management, he gave up, and the Théâtre de la Gaité went back for a time to the Offenbachanalian spectacle in which it had been before revelling.

Of late another attempt at the same theatre has been made. A company calling itself the Popular Opera is established at the Gaité, and is striving to get municipal recognition, and to have allotted to it an annual subvention, akin to the sum which first put the Théâtre Lyrique above the daily perils of a private enterprise calling for great daily outlay and relying on a wholly uncertain return.

Like the Théâtre Lyrique, the Porte St. Martin Theatre was burnt during the brief rule of the Commune. After the triumph of order, before it was rebuilt, a new Théâtre de la Renaissance was erected close to the site of the destroyed theatre. The new house, which architecturally is one of the prettiest and most notable in Paris, was intended originally for domestic and tragic drama. Here M. Émile Zola's first play failed. Indeed nearly everything attempted was either damned out of

THÉÂTRE DE LA RENAISSANCE.

hand or died slowly of inanition. Suddenly the theatre changed hands. The new manager was M. Victor Koning, one of the authors of "Mme. Angot's Daughter." The drama was ignominiously shown to the door, and the lightsome music of M. Lecocq and his fellows took its place.

Opéra bouffe will be duly considered in a later

chapter, and, in so far as the performances at the Théâtre de la Renaissance have been opéra bouffe, they may now be passed over. But while like to opéra bouffe in some respects, they were not opéra bouffe, but something which had grown out of opéra bouffe.

The visitor to Paris during the last Exhibition, who was also a visitor during the Exhibition of nine years before, could not but be struck by the difference of tone in the programmes presented for his consideration by the theatres of Paris. The form of entertainment which seemed so abundantly and so accurately to reflect the folly and the extravagance of the imperial days, opéra bouffe, was almost wholly invisible to those who have accepted the invitation of the Republic. During my stay of four weeks in Paris, not a single opéra bouffe appeared on the bills of any Paris theatre. M. Offenbach's " Orphée," it is true, was revived at the Gaité as a spectacular piece a few days after I left. The Bouffes, as its name indicates, the home of opera of this type, was closed. At the Renaissance the successful " Little Duke" of MM. Meilhac and Halévy, the authors of the "Grand Duchess," was avowedly an opéra comique, and M. Lecocq's music was altogether within the limits set by Auber and Hérold. At the Folies Dramatiques the even more successful "Chimes of Corneville" had, as we know in New York, far more of the characteristics of the opéra comique than of its extravagant younger sister. Whether this change, a real reform, was due to the advent of the Republic and of a consequent austerity of manners or not, it was welcome ; and, although the "Timbale d'Argent" and a few other outrageous indecencies have come into existence since the fall of the Empire, it seems as though the play-going Parisian public had experienced a change of heart.

A kindred change was to be seen in the theatres on the other side of the channel. Ten years ago most of the theatres in London were given up to loud sensation. Now the merely sensational play, while it has not wholly disappeared—it satisfies a certain portion of the theatre-going public too well to vanish utterly—has sunk to the subordinate position which it deserves, and the most successful theatres in London are those aiming at the proper all-round presentation of comedy, and taking as their model the Gymnase or the Vaudeville of Paris. From out of the empty and vapid burlesques has been developed a genuine English comic opera, neither opéra bouffe nor opéra comique ; the spirit of bouffe is foreign to English ways, and almost equally strange is the romantic grace of opéra comique.

The same years which have seen in France the development of the unclean opéra bouffe into the clean but still amusing opéra comique of M. Lecocq, saw in England the slow growth of the cheap burlesque into very amusing and genuine comic opera of the type of "Trial by Jury" and "H. M. S. *Pinafore*."

In Paris the leader in this change has been the Théâtre de la Renaissance, and it has been closely followed by the Folies Dramatiques, a little house for a long time given over to naked and blatant musical parodies like the "Little Faust" of M. Hervé. Of this new school, which is certainly not opéra bouffe, and which lacks the pretensions of the modern opéra comique—although it is probably not at all unlike what the opéra comique was in its earlier days—the best known examples are "Madame Angot's Daughter" and the "Little Duke," both composed by M. Lecocq, and the "Chimes of Corneville," by M. P. Planquette.

How great is the Parisian liking for music may perhaps be judged by this: in January, 1880, seven of the twenty-three most important theatres were giving operas, while at three others the plays, although not actually operatic, were full of songs.

CHAPTER V.

THE COMÉDIE-FRANÇAISE.

THAT the stage is in a better condition in France to-day than in any other country is hardly matter of dispute; and Paris is France, as far at least as the stage is concerned. It is not perhaps that there are more good actors in the French language than in English or German, but the good English-speaking actors are scattered broadcast over Great Britain and greater Britain, and the good German actors are divided here and there among the countless court theatres of the fatherland. The best of French actors are gathered into the half dozen best theatres of Paris; and the first company òf Paris is incomparably the finest company in the world. This company is the Comédie-Française, which acts at the Théâtre Français.

When Jean Baptiste Poquelin de Molière came to Paris, in 1658, at the head of the company of comedians who had been perfecting their playing during provincial wanderings for twelve years, and received from the king, Louis the Fourteenth, the title of "King's Company," and the promise of a pension of seven thousand livres a year, he found already installed in the city two other companies of actors. One was the company of the Marais theatre; the other occupied the Hôtel de Bourgogne, which it had derived in 1588 from the old Fraternities of the Passion, who had erected it in 1548 for the performance of the mysteries and farces which were then the only form of drama.

Molière's company, established at the Palais Royal, quickly surpassed in popular favor the Marais company; but between it and the Hôtel de Bourgogne there was bitter rivalry. The latter contained the best tragic actors; it was the elder, and it was the Royal Company. Molière's company was only the King's Company. Although it excelled easily in comedy, there seems now to be but little doubt that the elder theatre was generally considered the better. After Molière's death, in 1673, the Marais company united with his companions, and the rivalry continued—to the great disadvantage of the newly combined companies. Molière's company had of course acted all his comedies, and the Marais company had produced most of Corneille's; but, in spite of this record, the Hôtel de Bourgogne, headed by Mlle. Champsmélé, who had acted the heroines of most of Racine's tragedies, seemed likely to run its rival out of the field. But some internal dissension caused the secession of Mlle. Champsmélé and her husband, who joined the combined company of Molière's companions and the actors of the Marais. Shortly afterward, in 1680, the King arbitrarily decreed the union of the survivors of all three companies into one, and created thus by a simple royal decree the Comédie-Français, which still flourishes after a life of now two centuries. It is almost the only institution of royal France which survived the Revolution. Since it came into existence it has had no real rival; it has been always first in tragedy and first in comedy. Upon its boards nine out of ten of the great actors and actresses of the past two hundred years have played their parts. Upon its stage most of the best specimens of French dramatic literature have seen the light of the lamps for the first time.

To find any parallel for the career of the Comédie-Française in our language and literature we should have to rely on the imagination. If the Globe Theatre had been worthily maintained from Shakespeare's death until now; if the best works of Shirley and Congreve and Farquhar and Sheridan and Goldsmith had been written for it; if Barton Booth and Garrick and Siddons and Kemble and Kean had appeared on its stage; if our memory connected it with every masterpiece of dramatic writing and acting—then we might form some idea of the position held in Paris by the Comédie-Française.

Its influence upon the art of acting has been healthy, for although it has again and again contained actors of extraordinary merit, its aim has always been to present a play well performed throughout, and never to sacrifice the whole to a part, however brilliant the part might be. It has always been—to use the theatrical terms of to-day—a stock company, but a stock company generally having among its members half a dozen stars, and stars sometimes of extraordinary brilliancy. Adrienne Lecouvreur (whose career has since been taken as the basis of a play produced at this very theatre, with an actress quite her equal in the heroine's part); Lekain, the friend of Garrick; Talma, the friend of Kemble and the familiar of the great Napoleon; Mademoiselle Mars, the heroine of the earlier plays of Victor Hugo and Alexander Dumas, and last, but not least, Mademoiselle Rachel, whose rapid rise to the height of theatrical success, and whose fatal visit to this country are well remembered —all these were members of the Comédie-Française. It was the last of them, Rachel, who played, as only she could play, the touching story of one of the first of them, Adrienne Lecouvreur.

But not all great actors have belonged to it, nor have they always, if they have formed a connection with it, succeeded in making a place for themselves. Frédérick Lemaître, in some respects the foremost actor of this century, failed to hold his own at the Français. He was not scholarly enough, and he was not well enough schooled. Nor did Mme.

Dorval, who had acted with him again and again at the Porte St. Martin, stay at the Français long, although the one great part she had, she played with great effect. There was something wanting in both of them. The Théâtre Français required a classic refinement, which they, accustomed to melodramatic surroundings, failed entirely to convey. The theatre did not suit them, and they did not suit the theatre. But although a few bright lights of the French stage of to-day do not shine within its walls, never at any time in its history has the theatre had a stronger company than it has now. Never has it been able to present tragedy, or comedy, or even farce, with fuller effect than it can to-day.

Not only in actors, but in authors also, has the Théâtre Français been preëminent. From the three companies whose union called it into existence it inherited the traditions of the original performers in the great works of the classic period of French literature—the comedies and tragedies of Corneille, Molière, and Racine. In the next century it brought out the principal plays of Voltaire and of his rivals, and it gave a hearing to the two comedies of Beaumarchais, the "Barber of Seville" and the "Marriage of Figaro." During the Revolution and under the Empire dramatic literature slumbered, and indeed caused the few spectators to slumber also.

But with the Revolution of 1830 came the romantic revival which brought to the Théâtre Français many of the best dramas of M. Victor Hugo, of the elder Dumas, of Casimir Delavigne, and of Alfred de Vigny (from whose fine novel " Cinq Mars " Lord Lytton derived parts of his play of " Richelieu "). Within the past thirty years the comedies of Alfred de Musset, of Eugène Scribe, of M. Ernest Legouvé, of the younger M. Dumas, and of M. Émile Augier—the hardiest and healthiest of all modern dramatists—have in great part been first shown to the public by the Comédie-Française, or have been appropriated permanently by it after having been successful elsewhere. It is a principle with it to take to itself any good play or any good player who seems likely to suit its stage, wherever he or she or it may be. Many a play, after a successful run at the Odéon Théâtre or the Gymnase Dramatique, has been revived at the Français with renewed triumph. Many a time has an actor who was making the fortune of another theatre been taken away to itself by the long arm of the Comédie-Française, aided by the might of its ancient privileges and prerogatives.

The laws which govern the Théâtre Français are not to be found clearly stated anywhere. It is, in fact, a commonwealth—an association of actors governing itself, with a Lord Protector, as the manager may be called, appointed by the national authorities. As the nation owns the building of the

Théâtre, which it gives rent free, together with an annual subsidy of about fifty thousand dollars, it is no wonder that it claims some jurisdiction. Under the Bourbon monarchies it claimed even more. The gentlemen of the royal household exercised supervision over the royal theatre, and managed at various times to do a deal of petty mischief. In 1757, the rules governing the theatre were codified in forty articles, which defined the rights and duties of the associated actors toward each other, and toward the authors, employés, and all persons with whom they were connected in business.

Napoleon reconstructed the society in a famous decree, signed—characteristically enough—in 1812, in Moscow! Other decrees, notably those of 1850 and 1859, have modified this code, and, in fact, the Comédie-Française is now governed much as we are—by the common law; by a host of old customs universally respected. The associated actors are sharers in the profits—a custom which obtained in the time of Shakespeare and of Molière, and which is not without its effect in keeping down professional jealousy, and in preventing attempts at professional monopoly. This custom the Théâtre Français alone, of all French or English theatres, has kept up.

A committee of their number forms a sort of cabinet or advisory council for the director. Just what are the powers of the director or of the committee, if they should clash, it is impossible to say. In general, the director, if he is shrewd, and especially if he is successful, does about what he pleases. The present manager, M. Perrin, has been very successful, and he is in consequence allowed to carry things with a high hand. But an unsuccessful or unpopular director would probably find his movements so hampered by the committee and by the other associates that his resignation would be the only way out of the difficulty.

A young graduate of the Conservatory (the great national training school of actors and singers), who has taken a first prize, has the right to an appearance on the stage of the Théâtre Français. He is engaged at a salary by the year. If in time he should show marked ability, and give promise of becoming capable one day of playing the best parts in his line of business, he may be elected an associate—that is, a sharer in the management, in the profits, and in the responsibilities of the enterprise. The associates, who now number twenty-four, fill by election the vacancies in their ranks caused by retirement or death. The fair sex has here equal rights; the ladies vote, and are voted for; more than once has a majority of the associates been ladies.

But there are always more sharers than there are shares: there are now twenty-four *Sociétaires*, while there are never twenty shares available for this purpose. The young actor or actress begins, there-

M. COQUELIN.

fore, with an eighth or a quarter of a share, rising gradually, as his value to the theatre increases and vacancies are made by death or resignation, to a half, and finally to a whole share. M. Coquelin, the brilliant comic actor, was an associate for five years before he had a full share. Since M. Perrin has been the director of the theatre, the yearly yield of a share has been rapidly rising; in 1878 each full share paid a profit of forty thousand francs. As, however, the theatre may not make money, and the shares may be of no value whatsoever, each associate gets an annual salary proportionate to his merits, but much smaller than he would receive elsewhere. After a certain number of years of service, he may retire on a pension, varying in amount as he may have been of more or less value to the company. There are nearly always half a dozen valetudinarian actors and actresses living calmly and comfortably on the pension paid them by their younger comrades, as they themselves have once earned pensions for their elders. Certain of the profits are diverted each year to accumulate for the benefit of the associate when he retires; M. Bressant, for instance, when he withdrew from active service, received a lump-sum of eighty thousand francs, and is receiving an annual pension of eight or ten thousand more. Of course, the chance of profit is increased by the fact that the society, as I have said before, has its theatre from the government rent free; and its pensions are made certain by the ample government subsidy and by slowly-accumulated reserve funds.

The duties of the stage manager are divided among certain of the elder male associates, who assume them in turn for a week at a time; and for thus acting as *semainier* they get additional allowances. The task of these temporary stage managers is no light one. They are responsible for the acting. The routine duties of the position are discharged by a permanent official. In old plays the *semainiers*—to use the almost untranslatable French name—instruct the minor actors in the traditions of their parts, regulate all positions and bits of "business," and discuss thoroughly what shall be done. In modern plays they share this work with the author. For an important play there are sometimes as many as eighty rehearsals.

Besides his salary (and independent of his share of the possible annual profit, if he be an associate) each actor is paid a certain small sum every time he acts; thus the most useful and the most industrious are better paid than the lazy and less competent, and thus, too, the actor hesitates before refusing even an inferior part in a play which may be acted numberless times. In English and American theatres an actor is justified in refusing to play an unimportant part, as the public, seeing him in it night after night for perhaps six months, may forget that he is capable of better things; but at the Français the same piece is rarely played on two successive evenings, and never on three, and the actor who plays a poor part to-night knows that the next night he may have a better, or perhaps the best. This feeling leads to a generally higher level of acting; it gets more good players into one piece than is often possible with us.

At the Théâtre Français (to quote from a most instructive article which M. Sarcey contributed to the English review, *The Nineteenth Century*, last summer) "the most insignificant parts are filled, if not by first-class actors, at least by persons who have already studied long and know their business. In plays like 'Hernani' and 'Mademoiselle de Belle Isle,' for instance, there are a certain number of very secondary personages, some of whom have but a few words to utter, while others say nothing at all. These obscure parts, instead of being given up to common supernumeraries engaged for the night, are filled either by young actors who have their trial to go through, or by old actors who have no other talent but their perfect knowledge of the boards—in short, by actors who form part of the company, and who are thoroughly acquainted with the traditions and manners of the house."

The influence of the pernicious "star system" is so strong with us in America and in England that the London papers, commenting on the performances of the Comédie-Française in London during the summer of 1879, again and again spoke of Mlle. Sarah-Bernhardt as the "leading lady," and of M. Febvre or M. Mounet-Sully appearing "in support" of her. No terms could well be less exact. Mlle. Bernhardt is not a superior, therefore her comrades do not appear "in support;" she is not even the leading lady: she is simply an associate of the Comédie-Française.

On the playbills the names of the actors always appear in the order of their election as associates, the salaried actors following their seniors; in "Ruy Blas," for instance, the name of Mlle. Bernhardt, who plays the *Queen*, is preceded by that of Mlle. Jouassain, who acts the far less important part of the *Duenna*, because Mlle. Jouassain was elected an associate in 1863, and so is the senior of Mlle. Bernhardt, elected in 1875. There are no stars at the Théâtre Français, partly because the associates are all "stars," and partly because any individual prominence would break up the artistic unity which is the great beauty of the present organization. Rachel in her day was a "star," and the experience then gained will keep the Théâtre Français from ever repeating it. As M. Sarcey says: "Rachel cost the theatre more than she ever drew, and she did more harm to art than she rendered it service. . . . The nights on which she played, the receipts amounted to

M. FEBVRE.

10,000 francs, the whole of which went into her pocket. The next night the theatre was empty." On one occasion, when the bill contained "Tartufe" and the "Legacy," the masterpieces of Molière and Marivaux, the receipts were only sixty-seven francs. M. d'Heylli in his instructive "Journal Intime de la Comédie-Française," gives us the annual gross receipts of the theatre for the past thirty years. While Rachel acted they varied from about 300,000 francs to 900,000 (in 1855, the Exhibition year); from her death in 1858 to the war of 1870 they never fell below 800,000; after the war and the Commune they jumped to 1,262,000 in 1872, and rose steadily to 1,580,000 in 1877.

It will readily be seen that an institution as conservative as the Théâtre Français is likely to take little initiative in bringing out new authors. Its function is not to discover new dramatists and lead in dramatic progress, but to consecrate and reward acknowledged merit. Many of the plays which it now presents with great success were originally produced at other theatres—among them are the "Ciguë" and the "Gendre de M. Poirier" of M. Augier, and the "Demi-Monde" and "Fils Naturel" of M. Dumas. These and many other plays of a literary character won success elsewhere, a success which the Théâtre Français ratifies by taking them to itself. Its company is so much stronger than that of any other theatre of Paris, or even of any two others, that it is sure to act the piece better than it was originally acted.

It aims at a perfect performance of the masterpieces of French dramatic literature, old and new. Until 1867 the Théâtre Français had the exclusive right of presenting the classic drama, comic and tragic. The best plays of Molière, Racine, Corneille, and Beaumarchais are always in readiness, and are frequently performed. As the bill is changed nightly, a week rarely passes without one or more opportunities of seeing one of the classics (either light or heavy) of the French stage. A successful new play, like M. Augier's " Fourchambault " or M. Dumas's " Étrangère," is acted at first three or four times a week; then, as its attraction lessens, it is seen but twice, or even once a week. It does not finally drop out of the bill sometimes for two or three years, and it may then at any time be revived for another series of performances. It takes much longer for a play to attain its hundredth performance at the Français than elsewhere. But a good play there is above the chances of ill-luck, sickness of an actor, temporary lack of public interest, and so on, which beset it at other theatres. As the new play alternates with the play of last year, and of the year before, and as these alternate with the plays of two centuries ago, standards of comparison are supplied, and it is easier to judge a piece at its true value. The Théâtre Français is, in fact,

The Comédie-Française. 85

a museum of dramatic art, and as such it is fostered by the government. The subsidy is intended especially to provide for the proper performance of the classic drama, which has rarely been able to attract paying audiences. But the present director, M. Perrin, has been skilful enough to make Molière and Racine fashionable, and therefore as profitable as the latest new work of M. Augier or M. Dumas.

Here is the roll of the twenty-three associates of the Comédie-Française, with the date of the election of each one to the enviable dignity:

MM. Got . . . . (1850).
  Delaunay . . . . (1850).
  Maubant . . . . (1852).
  C. Coquelin . . . . (1864).
  F. Febvre . . . . (1867).
  Thiron . . . . (1872).
  Mounet-Sully . . . . (1874).
  Laroche . . . . (1875).
  Barré . . . . (1876).
  Worms . . . . (1878).
  E. Coquelin . . . . (1878).
Mmes. Madeleine Brohan . . . . (1852).
  Favart . . . . (1854).
  Jouassain . . . . (1863).
  Edile Riquier . . . . (1864).
  Provost-Ponsin . . . . (1867).
  Dinah Félix . . . . (1870).

Mmes. Reichemberg .... (1872).
Croizette .... (1873).
Sarah-Bernhardt .... (1875).
Barretta .... (1876).
Broisat .... (1877).
Jeanne Samary .... (1878).
Bartet .... (1880).

Besides these twenty-four associates there are sixteen salaried actors and eleven salaried actresses.

A glance at this list shows us that M. Got, the dean of the associates of the Comédie-Française, attained that dignity nearly the third of a century ago; and when we remember that he had served several years as a salaried actor before his election as an associate, we recall the question asked by M. Sarcey in the article from which quotation has already been made:

"Do you know that between Got and Molière there are only seven or eight names of great actors? We have, so to speak, only to stretch out our hand to be able, across several generations, to find the first *Mascarille*. Got played a long time with Monrose, who had seen Dazincourt. Dazincourt appeared young by the side of Préville, already old. Préville had known Poisson, who is the last link of the chain up to Molière. In this way the tradition has been preserved alive from one great actor to another. One feels how such or such a rôle was played in the days of Molière, and when by chance the interpretation is changed by the caprice of an actor, as happened in the case of *Arnolphe*, whose character was modified by the elder Provost, that change forms a date, and the new tradition is established, unless the successors of Provost reject it. Here we see the distinctive mark of the Comédie-Française, which unites to tradition a wise spirit of innovation that corrects and harmonizes it to the tastes of the day, but at the same time, out of respect for tradition, it always puts the bridle on this taste for novelty. The history of the Comédie-Française is only a perpetual compromise between these two contrary forces."

Just how much the old and the new are represented on the boards of the Théâtre Français can be seen by a few figures taken from the beautiful little dramatic annual the " Almanach des Spectacles." During the year 1878, the latest for which we as yet have the statistics, fourteen plays of Molière were acted in all seventy-seven times. Racine followed with five plays and twenty-four performances, and Corneille with four plays and fourteen performances. Five other classic plays, by Regnard, Marivaux, Voltaire, and Beaumarchais, were acted in all twenty-eight times.

Only one new modern play was brought out— the " Fourchambault " of M. Émile Augier. A formal revival was made of M. Dumas's " Natural

Son," hitherto acted at the Gymnase. Besides these two novelties, thirty-eight other plays, by thirty-three different modern authors, were acted on the stage of the Théâtre Français. Twenty-three of the pieces performed during the year were in five acts, and twenty-one had but one act.

This record is not wanting in variety; and when we remember that every play was acted as well as may be, and not in any way slighted, we may acknowledge that it is a record worthy of the Comédie-Française, and one which the Comédie-Française alone is capable of acquiring.

CHAPTER VI.

THE ACTRESSES OF THE COMÉDIE-FRANÇAISE.

WITHIN the past fifty years three great actresses —great indeed in different ways—have crossed the stage of the Théâtre Français, leaving a trail of glory behind them. The first was Mlle. Mars, who was almost equally at home in comedy, or tragedy, or drama. Of her, M. Legouvé, the author of "Adrienne Lecouvreur," tells an anecdote which sets her artistic skill in a strong light. One morning, at a rehearsal of "Louise de Lignerolles," one of M. Legouvé's earliest successes, in which she was to "create" the part of the heroine, she seemed tired and indisposed to exert herself. In the second act she had a scene which needed great energy, and M. Legouvé noted that she "rehearsed it without letting out her voice, making indeed hardly any gestures, and yet all the effects, all the intentions, all the shades of sentiment were expressed and visible. It was like a picture seen from afar, or like music heard at a distance. It suggested a pastel, slightly faded by time, but, in which every tone keeps its exact shade, every form holds its exact value, and everything, in short, was complete in proper proportion.

The little event was for me a revelation. I understood upon what a fixed basis the art of speech (*diction*) was founded, since a great artist could extinguish, if I may hazard the word, her personage, without making it lose anything in its proportions, in its *ensemble*, or in its relief."

Great exertion is not only unnecessary but injurious, as the speaker or reader, when once tired, has no reserve of strength at the moment when perhaps it is most needed. Talma, says M. Legouvé, condensed this into one striking maxim: An artist who fatigues himself is mediocre. How not to fatigue himself was only discovered by Talma after protracted experiment and infinite labor. A really great artist, indeed, rarely shrinks from labor, however long. M. Legouvé relates that he and Rachel, who was the second of these three great actresses, once spent three hours toiling over one line in this same " Louise de Lignerolles," in which Rachel was to follow, and hoped to surpass, her predecessor.

Rachel was not always so careful, or rather, having once mastered her parts, she was almost careless at times. Toward the end of her career, as Mr. Lewes informs us, she " played her parts as if only in a hurry to get through them, flashing out now and then with tremendous power, just to show what she could do ; and resembling Kean in the sacrifice of the character to a few points." In another part of his admirable little book on acting,

The Actresses of the Comédie-Française. 91

Mr. Lewes paid this tribute to the genius of the actress: "Rachel was the panther of the stage; with a panther's terrible beauty and undulating grace she moved and stood, glared and sprang. There always seemed something not human about her. She seemed made of different clay from her fellows — beautiful but not lovable. Those who never saw Edmund Kean may form a very good conception of him if they have seen Rachel. She was very much as a woman what he was as a man. If he was a lion, she was a panther."

Both Mlle. Mars and Mlle. Rachel are dead; the third artist is Mme. Arnould-Plessy, who is alive, although recently she has retired from the stage. She was the most polished and consummate of all actresses of comedy. As far as one may venture such a comparison, she must have resembled in style Mrs. Abington, who was the original *Lady Teazle*. But not content with her comedy triumphs, she chose one day to play *Agrippina* in Racine's tragedy "Britannicus." "I shall not say," wrote M. Sarcey in his next Monday's criticism, "that Madame Plessy is mediocre. With her intelligence, with her natural gifts, with her immense authority over the public, she could not in any way be mediocre. She is not therefore mediocrely bad. She is bad to an inexpressible degree." He then proceeded to prove his assertion. A few days later, finding Madame Plessy at a friend's house, he concealed himself as best he could, but she came straight to him, holding out her hand, while she smiled like a heroine of Marivaux. "You are right," she said; "you might have told the truth more amiably, but it was the truth. My friends and I were wrong, and I shall not again risk myself in a tragic part. I thank you." And, with a grand courtesy, she left him stupefied, for never in his twenty years' practice as a critic had he had such an experience.

There are no actresses now at the Théâtre Français of the value of Mlle. Mars, Mlle. Rachel, or Mme. Plessy. But the company at present contains two actresses who, whatever their artistic merits may be, are at least celebrities almost as famous as any one of their three great predecessors. These two ladies are Mlle. Sarah-Bernhardt, and Mlle. Sophie Croizette.

When Edwin Forrest was in Europe, in 1834 and 1835, he was called upon by the manager of a Paris theatre to give his opinion of an actor of whom the manager had great hopes. Forrest attended the performance, and told the manager afterward that the actor could never rise above respectable mediocrity. "But that Jewish-looking girl," he added, "that little bag of bones, with the marble face and the flaming eyes—there is demoniacal power in her. If she lives, and does not burn out too soon, she will become something wonderful." The prediction

MLLE. SARAH-BERNHARDT.

was fulfilled, for the Jewish-looking girl, the little bag of bones, was afterward known to the whole world as Rachel. For years after the death of Mlle. Rachel, there was no one to take her place at the Théâtre Français; there was no one to breathe into the hollow masks of French tragedy the breath of life, and to animate them into existence by the might of her genius. For years her place was vacant.

But within the past few years an aspirant has presented herself, whose claim for the honor is allowed by some of the most enlightened critics. The new-comer is also a little bag of bones, and has a Jewish-looking face. Like Rachel, Mlle. Sarah-Bernhardt is a Jewess. Her mother was of Dutch birth; her father was a Frenchman. She was educated in a convent, whence she was four times expelled for the trifles there regarded as mortal sins. It was only the tears and the singular charm of the child which conquered the hearts of the gentle sisters, and opened to her again and again the doors of the convent, which she finally left with many a prize. Once outside its walls and able to think of her future, she declared passionately her intention of being a nun—"unless," she added, after a second's pause, "unless I am an actress."

They sent her to the Conservatory. In due course of time she was graduated, and was engaged at the Théâtre Français. Here it was the usual story: there were but few parts for the beginner to make any impression on the public. Added to which, the impression made on the players by this reckless and restless personality was not altogether favorable; and when at last, for some good reason or other, she slapped the face of an associate—and an associate, too, of the fair and unforgiving sex—it was high time for her to leave the Comédie-Française, and she left it. After wandering here and there, even playing for a while in a spectacular play at the Porte St. Martin Theatre, she at last made an engagement at the Odéon Theatre, an establishment fostered by the government, partly as a nursery for the Théâtre Français. There she first appeared in 1867, and there she remained, playing parts of increasing importance, until, in 1872, she was again engaged at the Théâtre Français, to which she returned surrounded by a halo of eccentricity, and the heroine of a thousand anecdotes, few of them authentic, it may be, and all of them questionable.

She entered the theatre under protest, as it were, and at first failed. She had against her the regular supporters of the theatre, who regarded her eccentricities as but devices for notoriety, and she had few friends behind the curtain. But she fought her own battles, acting up to the motto—" *Quand-même.*" Mlle. Sarah-Bernhardt, like Rachel, con-

The Actresses of the Comédie-Française. 95

sumed by an inward fire, like Rachel again, believed in herself. And in time her turn came. In the "Sphinx," in which Mlle. Croizette played the vicious heroine, and made the judicious grieve by her

SARAH-BERNHARDT (SKETCHED BY HERSELF).

unduly sensational, not to say horrible, death scene, Mlle. Bernhardt played suffering and forgiving virtue; and, in the eyes of some judges, the real triumph of the evening was hers.

Her reputation began to grow rapidly. The fortunate revival of various tragedies, notably the "Zaïre" of Voltaire, gave her opportunities of which she made the most. She gave to tragedy a fire and a fervor to which it had been unused since Rachel had doffed the mantle of Melpomene. At last she dared even the memory of her great predecessor, and, as the *Phèdre* of Racine—perhaps the greatest of Rachel's great parts—she did not fail; in the opinion of a few of the young critics she even succeeded. The part, hard and trying, was doubly hard for so feeble an organization, debilitated by constant sickness. Dominating her weak body by sheer force of will, although she may spit blood and faint after each act, as she has done again and again, she never gives in.

After "Phèdre" and "Zaïre" came two new tragedies, the "Fille de Roland," and "Rome Vaincue," in each of which she bore off the honors. And in M. Dumas's "Étrangère" she again found herself face to face with Mlle. Croizette, and at first she again carried off the crown of victory; but as the play ran its due course Mlle. Croizette steadily improved on her first performance, which was at times careless. In one respect nature has favored Mlle. Bernhardt more than Mlle. Croizette. She is slight and slim of figure, while her competitor is rapidly becoming portly, and is even now of ample rotundity. A thin figure is ever more poetic than a stout one; and Mlle. Bernhardt is thin beyond all peradventure. She is indeed of such immaterial thinness that her attenuated figure is a stock subject for the professional jesters of Paris.

It is said, for instance, that she once escaped from robbers by hiding behind her riding-whip. It is said again, that, in her early career, a manager refused to engage her, alleging that he would not have in his theatre a woman who could enter his office through the keyhole. It is said, also, that when a picture of her, by M. Clairin, showing a noble hound reclining at her feet, was shown in the annual exhibition, M. Dumas, glancing at it, remarked, "I see—a dog and a bone!" But the utmost height to which this rather thin wit has gone as yet is the assertion that one evening an empty carriage drove up to the Théâtre Français and Mlle. Sarah-Bernhardt alighted from it.

In tragedy, and in the romantic heroines of the poetic drama, robed in the flowing and floating draperies of the mediæval or antique heroines, her long, thin figure gains dignity. It is in tragedy, too, that the marvellous and crystalline purity of her voice is most apparent. The unconscious beauty of her silver tones lends to the rhyming Alexandrines of French tragedy a value which they themselves do not always deserve. "You cannot praise her for reciting poetry well," says M. Théodore de Banville, a poet learned in metres and rhythms;

"she is the Muse of Poetry itself. A secret instinct moves her. She recites verse as the nightingale sings, as the wind sighs, and as the water murmurs."

When she left the convent, she hesitated between being a nun or an actress. When she was at last an actress, and perhaps the most notorious in France, she suddenly felt that she had missed her vocation, and that she was really intended for a sculptor. She called for modelling clay and the tools of the trade; she took a few lessons, and at the annual art exhibitions since, she has exhibited various pieces of sculpture of varying merit—not as amateurish and quite as startling as one might expect. Her latest attempt was a statue for M. Garnier's new opera-house at Monaco, which that clear-sighted architect peremptorily rejected. She passes all her days in her studio when she is not rehearsing or riding rapidly on horseback; but already, in spite of her success as a sculptor, has she turned her ever-restless intellect to the sister art of painting.

In all this there is a certain savor of merely meretricious sensationalism. The very thinness of which Mlle. Bernhardt complains is sometimes exaggerated wilfully by the costume she chooses, and gloves too full are deliberately wrinkled along the arms to increase the attenuated impression. In all the recklessness of character, in the sudden freak for sculpture and for painting, in the balloon trips described by herself at length in a volume profusely illustrated by M. Clairin, in the hastily dictated articles contributed to newspapers, in the eccentric caprices which give rise to strange tales of a skeleton in her studio, and of a coffin in which she sleeps, in the willingness to sacrifice to the impulse of the moment the demands of art, which must be steadily sought and long wooed ere it be won,—in all this there is evidence of conscious self-advertisement, not to say a distinct trace of charlatanry.

This unpleasant flavor was most prominent during the visit of the Comédie-Française to London in the summer of 1879. In a letter, written from London to the *Nation*, by an American writer, whom one cannot but suspect to be the critical author of "Daisy Miller," the extraordinary vogue of Mlle. Bernhardt in the English capital is considered with an insight as keen as its expression is charming.

"I speak," says this writer, "of her 'vogue,' for want of a better word; it would require some ingenuity to give an idea of the intensity, the ecstasy, the insanity, as some people would say, of curiosity and enthusiasm provoked by Mlle. Bernhardt. I spoke just now of topics, and what they were worth in the London system. This remarkable actress has filled this function with a completeness that leaves nothing to be desired; her success has been altogether the most striking and curious, although by no means, I think, the most gratifying, incident of the visit of the Comédie. It has not been the most gratifying, because it has been but in a very moderate degree an artistic success. It has been the success of a celebrity, pure and simple, and Mlle. Sarah-Bernhardt is not, to my sense, a celebrity because she is an artist. She is a celebrity because, apparently, she desires, with an intensity that has rarely been equalled, to be one, and because for this end all means are alike to her. She may flatter herself that, as regards the London public, she has compassed her end with a completeness which makes of her a sort of fantastically impertinent *victrix* poised upon a perfect pyramid of ruins—the ruins of a hundred British prejudices and proprieties. Mlle. Sarah-Bernhardt has remarkable gifts; her success is something quite apart, as the woman herself is something quite apart; but her triumph has little to do with the proper lines of the Comédie-Française. She is a child of her age—of her moment—and she has known how to profit by the idiosyncrasies of the time. The trade of a celebrity, pure and simple, had been invented, I think, before she came to London; if it had not been, it is certain that she would have discovered it. She has in a supreme degree what the French call the *génie de la réclame*—the advertising genius; she may, indeed, be called the muse of the newspaper. Brilliantly as she had already exercised her genius, her visit to

The Actresses of the Comédie-Française.

London has apparently been a revelation to her of the great extension it may obtain among the Anglo-Saxon peoples."

This is what an American critic thought of the woman. What an English critic — perhaps the most competent in his country to discuss French poetry, French drama, or French acting—thought of the actress, can be seen from this short extract from the very suggestive essay which Mr. Matthew Arnold wrote upon the French play in London:

"One remark I will make," writes Mr. Arnold, "a remark suggested by the inevitable comparison of Mlle. Sarah-Bernhardt with Rachel. One talks vaguely of genius, but I had never till now comprehended how much of Rachel's superiority was purely in intellectual power, how eminently this power counts in the actor's art as in all art, how just is the instinct which led the Greeks to mark with a high and severe stamp the Muses. Temperament and quick intelligence, passion, nervous mobility, grace, smile, voice, charm, poetry—Mlle. Sarah-Bernhardt has them all; one watches her with pleasure, with admiration, and yet not without a secret disquietude. Something is wanting, or, at least, not present in sufficient force; something which alone can secure and fix her administration of all the charming gifts which she has, can alone keep them fresh, keep them sincere, save them from perils by caprice, perils by mannerism;

that something is high intellectual power. It was here that Rachel was so great; she began, one says to oneself, as one recalls her image and dwells upon it—she began almost where Mlle. Sarah-Bernhardt ends."

The personality which to the majority of strangers would probably now—after Mlle. Sarah-Bernhardt—be the most interesting in the company of the Théâtre-Française is Mademoiselle Croizette. She it was who gave to the death-scene of M. Octave Feuillet's most unpleasant play so realistic a flavor, the fame of which crossed the Atlantic and made the name of the actress familiar in America. Mlle. Sophie Croizette is a child of the stage; her grandfather was dramatic author and actor and manager; his daughter (her mother) was a dancer. Her father was a Russian, and she was born in St. Petersburg about thirty years ago. She shows in her acting a certain strange savor of her Slav ancestry, as well as an air of coquetry truly Parisian. Her mother, who had in all three daughters, did not wish any of them to go on the stage; she has received two-thirds of her wish; one of her daughters has quietly married a merchant, another is the wife of M. Carolus Duran, the artist, and only the third went on the stage, where she has won a remarkable success.

She was carefully educated as a governess, passing with honors the government examinations, and

MLLE. CROIZETTE (AFTER M. CAROLUS DURAN).

gaining a knowledge of music and a mastery of the piano, which have been of great service to her since. The severity of the examinations broke down her health, and she had a long sickness. Even after this she still looked too young and too slight to be trusted with the important work of teaching. She could find nothing to do. Her two sisters married, and she was left alone restless at her uselessness. An intimate friend of her mother's, a retired actress, constantly talking about the stage, awakened what speedily became an irresistible desire, and at last, by the aid of M. Bressant, then one of the leading actors of the Théâtre Français, but now retired, she was admitted to the Conservatory. In France no one thinks of taking to the stage hastily, and acting in "The Hunchback" or "Romeo and Juliet" after half a dozen lessons. The difficulties of the art of acting are better appreciated there, and the preparatory work of a pupil at the Conservatory is long and toilsome.

Mlle. Croizette remained there two years, being graduated at last with the first prize—which opened to her the doors of the Théâtre Français. Just at this time "Frou-frou" was seeking an actress for its heroine, and the authors and the manager of the Gymnase Dramatique, where it was to be produced, thought they saw in Mlle. Croizette the actress that the part required. But the Comédie-Française conquered; Mlle. Croizette was engaged at an annual salary of eighteen hundred francs, which was raised to three thousand four hundred the night of her first appearance. "Frou-frou" found a finer interpreter than the raw novice could then have been, in the late Mlle. Desclée, by far the greatest actress of the last ten years, whose early death is deeply to be deplored by all lovers of the dramatic art.

For two years Mlle. Croizette played various parts in the regular repertory—the thirty or forty, or even at times more plays, some of which are acted two or three nights a week to give relief to the monotony of the current novelty. In January, 1873, she was elected an associate, and in July came her first opportunity, and she made the most of it. The play was but one single little act long, but this was enough. It was the "Été de la St. Martin" of MM. Meilhac and Halévy, the authors of "Frou-frou," who had compounded for her a part of singular and seductive grace, admirably adapted to her personal and peculiar charms.

After this came a rather more important part character in M. Augier's drama made from the fine novel, "Jean de Thommeray," of his friend M. Jules Sandeau—using with most picturesque effect the Franco-Prussian war as a background. In this part Mlle. Croizette was again successful. Not long after she was intrusted with the leading part in M. Octave Feuillet's peculiar play, the

The Actresses of the Comédie-Française. 107

"Sphinx." The part was identical with the rather romantic heroine of any other of M. Feuillet's plays, but Mlle. Croizette endowed it with a nameless fascination, a subtle and almost barbaric color, serving as a fit preface for the curious catastrophe. The motto of Mlle. Croizette is *à outrance*—to the death, to the bitter end; and the style in which she treated the final scene of M. Feuillet's play shows how she actèd up to her motto. The plot required that she should die by poison, and the author intended no undue dying struggle, but a quiet and simple death. Mlle. Croizette elaborated the situation into a "sensation" which made a pecuniary success for the play, although it degraded the play-house by turning it for a time into a chamber of horrors.

There was in the theatre a general feeling of disgust at the spectacle, and one sharp hiss was heard; but, as has been said, the death-scene was the "sensation" of the piece, which it saved from dying of inanition. It was town talk, and it gave to the actress a notoriety which has attracted to her and to her subsequent parts an attention which her merits, real and remarkable as they are, would never have sufficed to attract. Since the "Sphinx," Mlle. Croizette has appeared in several old plays and in one new part, the *Duchess* in M. Dumas's "Étrangère." In this she eschewed sensational devices; she embroidered it with no clap-trap and catchpenny tricks; relying for success purely on her undoubted histrionic powers, she gained another triumph, not as loud-sounding as its predecessor, but more worthy, and probably more appreciated by the actress herself.

Just as Jules Janin discovered Rachel, so M. Sarcey, in a measure, discovered Mlle. Bernhardt. His was the word of encouraging criticism which greeted her early appearances, and his the phrases of glowing eulogy which awaited her triumphs. But M. Sarcey, although an admirer, is, above all, a critic, and he has not hesitated to declare that Mlle. Bernhardt's range is very limited. The lyre may be divine, yet it has but one cord. Now here Mlle. Croizette has the advantage of Mlle. Bernhardt. Her talent is far more supple; it bends itself more readily to a greater variety of parts. She is a far more useful actress in the theatre than Mlle. Bernhardt, although of late her usefulness is beginning to be somewhat circumscribed by her growing amplitude of figure.

In London, the easy-chair provided for her to fall back in at the end of the startling scene at the end of the "Sphinx" was not large enough. The actress almost fell to the floor, and of course her point was spoilt. This fulness of figure begins to debar Mlle. Croizette from those juvenile and girlish parts in which she first became known. It is forcing her into the stronger and more mature heroines of high comedy; and a transition period is always an ungrateful one.

It is fourteen years now since I first went to the Théâtre Français, and although I was only a lad then, I can remember distinctly the performance that evening and the effect it had upon me. The chief play on the programme was the beautiful and pathetic " On ne badine pas avec l'amour" (" No Trifling with Love ") of Alfred de Musset; and I do not think I can ever forget the thrill which ran through me at the final words of the last scene, grandly played by M. Delaunay and Mlle. Favart, then at her best, and delivering with great effect the irrevocable " Farewell, Perdican: she is dead!"

The coming of Mlles. Bernhardt and Croizette has had the effect of pushing somewhat into the background Mlle. Favart, who, for ten years or more, had worthily held the head of the company. Time will not wait or go more slowly even for the leading lady of the leading theatre of the world, and Mlle. Favart is beginning to discover that youth is even better than experience. Was it not Mrs. Siddons who said that no woman ever knew enough to play " Juliet" until long after she was too old to look it? Mlle. Favart is an actress of consummate art, but she is no longer young enough to look the juvenile heroines she is otherwise so competent to act; and wiser in her generation than Mlle. Mars—who held on with a grip of iron to the girlish parts she had played for forty years, until, at last, some heartless ruffian threw a wreath of immortelles upon the stage at her feet—Mlle. Favart is of late beginning to accept the inevitable. She is therefore taking up parts in which her skill and experience will tell—parts like the mother in Mme. de Girardin's touching little play, "La Joie fait Peur" (Irished for us by Mr. Boucicault as "Kerry; or Night and Morning"). Mlle. Favart has thus passed from the playing of the heroines to the playing of the hero's mother.

Among the other ladies of the Comédie Française are Mlle. Jouassain, who plays comic old women, and Mme. Madeleine Brohan, daughter and sister of actresses like her, clever, beautiful, and witty, having indeed her full share of the well-known wit of the family, and bearing as proudly as they the family motto. As the old Rohan declared, "*Roi ne puis; Prince ne daigne; Rohan suis,*" so, paraphrasing this, Mlle. Brohan said at her first appearance, "*Mars ne puis; Plessy ne daigne; Brohan suis.*"

Mlle. Brohan is most charming to gaze at, and, in spite of an indolence which has prevented her from taking the high rank to which her natural ability entitles her, she appears to the utmost advantage in witty and amiable dowagers, ladies of the old school, puncturing more modern pretensions with a swift epigram, and sometimes putting aside more

MLLE. FAVART.

modern notions with a graceful wave of her antique fan.

Besides these elderly ladies, there is a bevy of younger beauties—not all of them beauties either; but nearly all graduates of the Conservatory, with native talent, good training, and high hopes. Chief among them is Mlle. Suzanne Reichemberg, the leading *ingénue*, if a French word may be used which has no exact English equivalent. An *ingénue* is the fresh and innocent young girl unawakened as yet to the wickedness of the world—a character French authors are fond of drawing, and therefore frequent in French dramatic literature from Molière's day to ours. Mlle. Baretta plays the same line of parts, but she lacks the largeness of style which characterizes Mlle. Reichemberg's acting in the classic comedies. Nor is Mlle. Reichemberg confined to the old plays: her greatest success has been as *Suzel*, in the "Friend Fritz" of of MM. Erckmann-Chatrian, a part which her Alsacian ancestry may have helped her to fill satisfactorily. Mlle. Baretta's dainty and delicate ways, which lend a charm to pretty little plays of our day, are at fault in the fuller and freer outlines of the older plays, and in these Mlle. Reichemberg is easily the superior. But there is about Mlle. Baretta a certain outspoken frankness of style not without its charm and its merit.

Between Mlles. Bernhardt and Croizette in the

leading parts, and Mlles. Baretta and Reichemberg in the younger characters, comes Mlle. Broisat, who, in spite of the unexpected favor with which she was received in England, has never in Paris been considered other than a useful and competent actress, capable of good work in second-rate parts.

The *soubrettes*, or pert waiting-women of classic comedy, of no slight importance in many of Molière's best plays, are divided at the Théâtre Français between Mlle. Dinah Félix, a sister of Rachel, and Mlle. Jeanne Samary, a niece of Mlle. Brohan.

In the month of February, just as this little book was trying to get itself into print, a new and important comedy, in five acts, by M. Victorien Sardou, and called " Daniel Rochat," was brought out at the Théâtre Français, with Mlle. Bartet in the chief part. It was the second time that M. Sardou ventured on the stage of the Théâtre Français. His first play at this house was a hopeless failure; but now, having recently been elected a member of the French Academy, he held it a point of honor to make his first appearance before the public on the stage of the Théâtre Français. And at his request Mlle. Bartet was engaged. A graduate of the Conservatory, and still very young, Mlle. Bartet had her first triumph in the trying part of *Zicka*, in M. Sardou's " Dora," in some respects his strongest and finest work, and known to the English and American stage as " Diplomacy." Her part in

"Daniel Rochat" was more prominent and important, and even though the new drama fail, her position in the theatre hereafter will be secure, and the Comédie-Française will have gained a valuable acquisition. At present, as we have seen, there is no actress at once young and clever, who is capable of playing brilliantly the youthful heroines of modern comedy. These were the parts that Mlle. Favart played before she began to show signs of age, and that Mlle. Croizette acted before she bloomed out into her present matronly majesty of figure.

Mlle. Bartet comes just in the nick of time, if the rumor be true, which reports that Mlle. Favart is about to take her retreat, resigning from the company of which she was long a leader, and retiring on the ample pension her services have secured her. It is possibly Mlle. Favart's resignation that has made the vacancy in the ranks of the associates which Mlle. Bartet has, since the first performance of "Daniel Rochat," been elected to fill.

CHAPTER VII.

THE ACTORS OF THE COMÉDIE-FRANÇAISE.

CUSTOM has created, in comedy and drama, certain recognized classes of characters. An actor who devotes himself to one line of parts expects to receive all the parts of that line. In a very full company there would be a pair of "leading men," a "light comedian," an "old man," a couple of "low comedians," an actor of "character," or eccentric parts, a "heavy man"—the villain of the piece—and a "walking gentleman." There would be a pair of "leading ladies," a "juvenile lead," an "*ingénue*," a "chamber-maid," an "old woman"—perhaps two. These are the more important people which a full and first-rate company would require. In its twenty-three associates, each sharing in the profits and playing the best parts in his or her line, the Comédie Française has more actors and actresses of the first rank than have ever anywhere else been gathered into one company—not excepting even the wonderful conjunction of comedians who formed the cast of the original "School for Scandal."

This classification is not rigid. It often happens that, owing to special circumstances, the "low comedian" takes the part of an old man, or the "character" actor is cast for a "heavy" part. No hard-and-fast rules can be laid down. All precedent yields before the diversity of talent exhibited by the different actors holding technically the same rank and the same line of parts. In the Théâtre Français, M. Coquelin is one of the "low comedians;" but in the "Étrangère" of M. Dumas, M. Coquelin created the part of the *Duke of Septmonts*, the aristocratic villain of the piece; and when the play was adapted to the American stage this same rascally *Duke* was played here by Mr. Coghlan, the "leading man" of the theatre. And again, in the "Fourchambault" of M. Emile Augier, the greatest success of the Exposition year, and an honest and hardy play, the two strongly contrasted and pivotal parts of the piece are played by M. Got and M. Coquelin. Now, M. Got and M. Coquelin are both technically "low comedians;" they both act, or have acted, the intriguing serving-men of Molière's comedies—the *valets de Molière*, as the parts are called; and these were the parts Molière wrote for himself, and to play them in Molière's own house is no small honor. Indeed, one well-known French actor is said to have refused an engagement at the Théâtre Français, because he did not wish to enter a house where the valets were the masters.

Before MM. Got and Coquelin, the parts were held by M. Samson, the tutor of Rachel, and by M.

Regnier, the teacher of both of his successors. And no one of these four remarkable comedians limited himself to the parts which came strictly within his technical line. M. Coquelin — to cite again the actor of at once the greatest promise and the finest performance on the French stage of to-day — acts, outside of his own line, the villains in the "Fourchambault" and the "Étrangère," the suffering and hungry ballad-maker in M. Théodore de Banville's beautiful "Gringoire," and the revolutionary hero of "Jean Dacier."

Of the three first and foremost actors now at the Théâtre Français, M. Got, M. Delaunay, and M. Coquelin — to name them in the order of seniority — two are essentially, as has been said already, comic actors. With these two a review of the male performers of the Comédie Française must perforce begin.

Although M. Got is the dean of the Comédie-Française, or, in other words, the senior associate, he is not yet an aged man. As an artist no one is less old. M. Got seizes on the modernness of a part, accentuates it, and gives you a palpitating actuality, as the French call it, meaning thereby a pertinence to the things of to-day. But when the part is not modern, when it is a figment of the imagination, a fantastic fashioning, M. Got gives full play to his own abundant fantasy, and revels in the rich humor and the rioting farce. When he

M. GOT.

has to copy reality, he copies it with an exactness and a relief simply astonishing. And it is in parts of this class that he has made his greatest successes. The authority over the public which he now exerts was not gained without toil and weary waiting. He was a charity scholar, taking prizes by hard work, until an insult from a coarse superior made him give up his studies, and, at the age of eighteen, take to journalism.

Then he went to the Conservatory, winning a prize with an annual allowance, which stopped when he was graduated with the highest honors. For a time he supported himself as a bookseller's hack, until he drew a bad number in the conscription and fell into the ranks, a private in the army. Eight months later he was a sergeant. This not satisfying his ambition, he applied for permission to make a first appearance at the Comédie-Française, to which his prize at the Conservatory entitled him. His first appearance was a bad failure. Two days later, he read in a paper a slashing article on his acting, and by accident the same night he met the writer of it, one Charles Maurice, a clever free lance, or freebooter rather, whose weapon was ever for sale.

"Well, young man," said he to Got, "why have you not been to see me? In France it is customary for an artist to call on a writer to thank him for kindly criticism."

"In fact, sir," said Got, "I am poor, and I have no money to pay the *claque*."

The venomous journalist never forgave the actor; he was Got's bitterest enemy—to Got's great profit, for, as he told M. Sarcey, " Maurice had a marvellous skill in finding weak places, and an incomparable meanness in railing at them. I corrected myself of many a fault by reading his criticism, and it cost me nothing. It was all clear gain." This shows just what stuff the actor was made of; he criticised himself; he toiled, he studied, he improved; and when M. Augier wrote his "Effrontés," M. Got, who in the meantime met with not a few successes, attained an overwhelming triumph. From philosophic comedy to the most extravagant farce is a wide range, but M. Got takes it all in. No more thoughtful, contemplative actor exists anywhere, but in farce he carries absurdity to the very climax of extravagance, without once losing his grip of himself or his audience.

The portrait of M. Got in the part of *Maître Pierre Pathelin*, given in this book, was copied from the etching prepared for M. Sarcey's "Comédiens et Comédiennes." It is fitting that the oldest associate of the Comédie-Française should be pictured in a character of the oldest extant play of the French language. Competent critics of acting have praised especially the exuberant and tremendous comicality with which he carries off this relic of mediæval farce. The play itself has had adventures enough to furnish forth one of the most extended and interesting chapters of literary history, which, if a digression be pardoned, may be briefly summarized here.

It was written in the fifteenth century, possibly by the famous François Villon, but more probably by Pierre Blanchet. Saturated in situation and language with Gallic salt, it was the most popular farce of the century, and doubtless received additions on all sides; it was imitated by Reuchlin in Germany, and one of its most important scenes is to be found in the "Towneley Mysteries." The familiar phrase "Revenons à nos moutons" had its origin in the action of this play, and many a French proverb is first to be found in it. Both Molière and La Fontaine admired its frank gayety. But after their death comedy stiffened, and the frantic farce was worked over into a mild three-act comedy—"L'Avocat Pathelin," by Brueys and Palaprat, which held the stage for nearly two hundred years, and only left it because M. Edouard Fournier, in 1872, brought out a reverent revision of the original text, far more racy and idiomatic than the watered comedy whose usurpation it ended. Another modification of the old farce has been set as a comic opera.

It was, however, "L'Avocat Pathelin" which served as a basis for "The Village Lawyer," a two-act farce produced by Garrick in London, at Drury Lane Theatre, with the usual success, and a rather more lasting success than most of Garrick's productions, for the play may be said almost to hold the stage to this day, as it has been played here in New York, by Mr. Jefferson, within twenty years. Nor is this the last of the play's transformations. In those places of amusement which for some inscrutable reason are called "variety" shows, is frequently given "an Ethiopian sketch," in two scenes, called "The Mutton Trial," which is a perversion of "The Village Lawyer;" and thus traces of the oldest specimen of French dramatic literature are still to be seen on the American stage.

The actor who shares with M. Got the more comic parts is M. Coquelin. It is hard to say which is the greater. M. Got is the elder soldier, and has therefore been first considered. M. Coquelin has finer natural advantages. For one thing he has a voice of extraordinary strength and brilliancy; he plays each of his parts in a different key, a different color, as it were, and when he has once begun he gives it no further thought, so thoroughly has training made it obedient to his will. M. Coquelin has youth—he is not forty; he has fire and fervor; he has a quick intelligence and great ambition; he has studied hard and in the best school; but the quality which strikes one at first hearing him is his ringing and sonorous voice, revelling in trumpet notes and rolling out a long speech with unbroken felicity.

After M. Coquelin had been graduated from the Conservatory, and had entered the Français, he was assigned a part in a new play. His delight was but short, for the author, to oblige an old actor, Provost, gave it to Provost's son. To console M. Coquelin for his disappointment, the manager offered him, novice as he was, the choice of a part. He chose *Figaro*, the valet in the "Marriage of Figaro," and for four acts he was so frightened that everything failed him: but in the fifth act he recovered himself and conquered his audience, and from that time to this no one has disputed his title to the whole line of valets. In many other parts in Molière's plays, although especially in the valets, which he fills with a rushing and turbulent gayety absolutely irresistible, M. Coquelin has been successful, imprinting on each a definite individuality.

Of late, M. Coquelin has chosen to try for tears as well as laughter. They lie perilously close together. But the actor knew his powers, and won new laurels in a new field. Some of the best of his later parts mingle tears and smiles—notably in the "Tabarin" of his friend, M. Paul Ferrier, one of the most promising of the younger dramatists of France. In this play he is represented as married, and he and his wife belong to a company of mountebanks. The great scene of the piece shows us the stage of the strolling company, with *Tabarin* playing the part of a deceived and abandoned husband. While he is amusing the crowd with his droll grief, he discovers that his wife actually has eloped. His feeling breaks at once through the paint of the clown, and he weeps real tears, but the silly crowd applaud only the more, and cannot see the breaking heart beneath. It may be imagined what opportunity such a part affords to an actor, and what advantage M. Coquelin takes of it.

His interest in M. Ferrier's play is none the less for the fact that the piece was written under his eye and at his suggestion—the author's original intention having been to use the situation in the libretto of a grand opera, in which M. Faure, the great baritone, should sing *Tabarin.*

Another play which M. Ferrier has written for M. Coquelin is called " At the Lawyer's," and shows a quarrelling husband and wife meeting in the presence of the man of law. It is a comic treat to see Mlle. Sarah-Bernhardt trying to vie in volubility with M. Coquelin, before the face of the astonished lawyer, who cannot get in a word edgeways.

In M. Dumas's latest play, the " Étrangère," he is shown in still another class of character: here he is a villain of the deepest dye, but of the utmost polish and the noblest birth. The *Duke* is a choice specimen of the ultimate corruption to which an enervated aristocracy is liable. The *Duke* is outwardly a perfect gentleman, and inwardly the most despicable of wretches. In the play, which, by the way, is not one of M. Dumas's best, although in the *Duke* we have one of M. Dumas's boldest and most satiric portraits, there is an American to whom the *Duke* makes a dishonorable proposition, and who leads the Duke on by tacit acquiescence in his schemes until he sees the extent of their villany and meanness. Then he turns and tells the *Duke* that he has made a mistake in thinking that he could take a hand in any dirty job like this, and he ends by sharply shaking his finger in the *Duke's* face and threatening him with summary and condign punishment if he dare to proceed with his plans. I know of nothing finer on the modern stage than the expression of M. Coquelin's face as he listened to this speech—surprise at the unusual tone, doubt as to whether the words could be meant for him, growing conviction that the fellow was insolent, rapidly rising anger, and a final outburst, with the sudden exit to fight a duel to the death off-hand then and there.

But a truly great actor is greatest in the greatest part, and perhaps M. Coquelin is seen at his best in the rich comic characters of Molière's noble comedies. He is the ideal *Mascarille*—quick-witted, light-fingered, loud-mouthed, and long-winded. And he is scarcely less admirable as the timid servant of

"Don Juan," or in the three or four different parts he chooses to play in "Les Facheux." Upon him more than upon any one other rests the future of classic comedy at the Théâtre Français.

The brilliant correspondent of the *Nation*, from whose letter, written in London during the summer of 1879, while the Comédie-Française were on their visit to England, quotation has already been made, brought his epistle to an end with a striking paragraph which sums up at once justly and effectively M. Coquelin's merits:

"The striking thing in London, however, as it has long been in Paris, is the great superiority of the masculine side of the house. The great trio of Got, Delaunay, Coquelin, is unapproached, and from present appearances unapproachable, by any feminine combination. Each of these great actors has won himself large honors with the English public; each of them has done with a rich perfection that which he has had to do. If I were to put forward one of these artists rather than another as the source of my own highest pleasure, I think I should have little hesitation in naming the rich, the rare, the admirable and inimitable Coquelin. There was a time when I thought Got the first of living actors, and Got is certainly still a consummate, a superb comedian. But as Coquelin has advanced in life and in his art, he has attained a command of his powers and developed an intelligence of the whole dra-

M. DELAUNAY.

matic mystery which place him, to my sense, almost alone. His variety, his versatility, the extent of his scale, are extraordinary; he is at once the most joyous and exuberant of pure comedians and the most powerful and touching of serious actors. He has a deeper intelligence than is often seen upon the stage; he strikes at once the note of high comicality and the note of passion, of deep seriousness; and he does both of these things with a certain touching, moving, exciting ardor. I said just now that Mlle. Sarah-Bernhardt was supposed to be going to America. That is all very well; but what I really wish is that M. Coquelin would go."

The third of the three great actors of the Comédie-Française to-day—and indeed it may well be doubted if in all its history it has ever had three finer artists playing constantly together—and the second of them in point of seniority, is M. Delaunay. In speaking of Mlle. Favart in the preceding chapter I have recorded the profound impression made on me the first time I saw M. Delaunay. The admiration then excited has deepened with every opportunity since offered to observe his grace, his ever-present youth, and his consummate skill. A more perfect artist than M. Delaunay it would be impossible to find. He plays the young lovers, the Orlandos who hang sonnets on trees, and breathe tender messages of love to the whispering winds. He has a beautiful, clear, silvery voice, which he uses with wonderful effect. To have seen him and Mlle. Favart a few years ago as the *Poet* and the *Muse* in Alfred de Musset's rhapsodic reverie, "The October Night," is to have seen that which it is an ever-recurring pleasure to recall.

He is good-looking, and he is young-looking. Although a little over fifty, no one who saw him for the first time in a youthful part would ever credit him with more years than the part called for. But he himself knows his advancing age, and he has already turned his attention to heavier parts, for which his skill and his natural gifts fit him, and which he would before have taken up had there been any one to replace him as the lighter lovers. There is no danger that he will ever be hissed for appearing in a part for which he was incapacitated by senility; no danger that the shrill sound will make him come to the foot-lights as once it did Mlle. Mars, to say in self-defence: " Messieurs, Mlle. Marie"—her part in the play—" is but sixteen years old. Mlle. Mars, alas! is sixty!"

M. Delaunay is seen at his best in the elegant and light-headed lovers, like the hero of Molière's "Étourdi," or in the quick-witted and lying lovers, like the hero of Corneille's " Menteur "—a hero, this last, whom we have had preserved for us here by Mr. Lester Wallack's clear-cut performance in Mr. Charles Mathews's reduction of Foote's " Liar." It is in these richly endowed and poetically imagined characters that he is most at ease, and this suggests the other side of the medal. He is always ideal, and rarely real in the sense of to-day. He is best in the graceful mantle of classic comedy. He is even almost ill at ease in the frock coat and trowsers of hard and complex modern comedy. Indeed, he is not modern. Even in a comedy of the nineteenth century he cannot rid himself of the grace and the charm and the amplitude of the comedy of the seventeenth century. In this respect he is in complete contrast to M. Got, his only senior as an associate, who, as has already been remarked, is the very incarnation of modernness.

In the suggestive biographical sketch which M. Sarcey has drawn of this actor, he says that M. Delaunay's life can be summed up in the single phrase, "Associate of the Comédie-Française." Graduated from the Conservatory with a prize in 1845, he acted for two years and a half at the Odéon, the second Théâtre Français, and in 1848 he crossed the river to join the Comédie-Française, of which he was made an associate in 1850. For the noble institution, in the history of which for now more than thirty years he has borne an honorable part, M. Delaunay has the highest respect and reverence. It grieves him to see any scandals or bickerings clouding even for a moment the fair fame of the Comédie-Française. Holding that to be a member of the organization founded by Molière is the highest honor to which an actor can aspire, he regards with no slight dissatisfaction those of his comrades who are not content with their shares of the liberal profits lately divided among the associates, but seek to enlarge their gains by a multitude of external engagements—a recitation here and a little comedy there.

M. Delaunay reserves himself for the service of his art, and of the Comédie-Française; except for charity, he rarely if ever appears as an actor elsewhere. There is no possible flavor of charlatanry about M. Delaunay, and there is nothing of which, one might infer, he would more disapprove than the gratutious self-advertisement of Mlle. Sarah-Bernhardt, degrading alike to art, to the artist, and to the company to which she belongs. Any one familiar with the history of the Théâtre Français, and with its traditions, cannot but feel that personages like Mlle. Sarah-Bernhardt are very much out of place within its walls. It is well that there are yet some like M. Delaunay, who hold firmly to the traditions of the institution, and who uphold nobly the dignity of the art of which they are professors.

It is scarcely possible to imagine a greater contrast to the tender and poetic M. Delaunay than the impulsive M. Mounet-Sully. It is the contrast of art and nature. And, on the stage, what is needed is not nature, raw and fresh, but art; that

M. MOUNET-SULLY.

is to say, nature artistically revealed and presented. And M. Mounet-Sully, who probably considers himself a "natural" actor, gives us at best but an expression of his own personality.

It may be doubted whether M. Mounet-Sully, who plays the fiery and impassioned heroes of drama and tragedy, and who is altogether a very remarkable young man, is deserving of mention before M. Frédéric Febvre, who may be—indeed is—the truer artist. But M. Mounet-Sully is the only young actor of prominence in the Comédie-Française who has any touch of the poetic spirit, and who is in any way capable of playing the perfervid heroes of French Alexandrines. For this reason, if for no other, he deserves mention immediately after M. Delaunay.

It is also to be said that M. Mounet-Sully, though less of an artist than M. Febvre, has greater natural gifts. He is the born actor, not the made actor, and certainly not the actor who, born with genius, has strengthened it by study. He can act merely as he feels, and his feelings change from day to day. He rarely plays the same part twice alike, and this is a sure sign of imperfect art; for when an actor has once found the proper emphasis, the proper tone, and the proper gesture for a phrase, he should always seek to give the phrase just that emphasis, just that tone, and accompany it by just that gesture. At one time he may be able to do it more effectively than another, but he should always try to do this. To this fundamental principle of the art of acting, which all great actors have complied with, M. Mounet-Sully cannot conform. He cannot think out a part in all its details, and gain a mechanical mastery over them, leaving his mind free to the full effect of his emotion. He is only good when the part exactly suits his oriental and barbaric, and somewhat ferocious, temperament.

In modern comedy, in the drama of every-day life, he was at first wellnigh insupportable. M. Emile Augier gave him the leading part in his "Jean de Thommeray," and had great difficulty in drilling him in the necessary action of the part. What he acquired to-day he lost to-morrow. "Great heavens!" cried the exasperated author, at last, "try to have a little less genius and a little more talent!"

M. Frédéric Febvre is only one of the first-rate actors at the Théâtre Français who appears to advantage solely in modern plays. As a Frenchman and a critic said of him to me, "He cannot play the repertory!" Now, as almost as many performances of old plays as of new are given every year in the Théâtre, this inability to take part in the classic drama is a decided drawback to the actor. It comes, in a measure, from the fact that M. Febvre is not a graduate of the Conservatory, but is altogether a self-taught actor, who has got his training as best he could, at first in the provinces, and afterward here and there in the theatres of Paris.

In M. Légouvé's little book on the art of reading, much importance is attached to *diction*, a word which has no exact English equivalent, "delivery" being perhaps the closest synonym. M. Sarcey recurs again and again to *diction;* it is a quality indispensable at the Théâtre Français, where many if not most of the plays are in verse, abounding in sonorous lines. This skill in delivery is either a natural gift, as in the case of Mlle. Sarah-Bernhardt, or it is only acquired in the Conservatory, whence most of the actors of the Théâtre Français have graduated. It is not so much needed at the other theatres, and when an actor from them comes to the Français, he often finds out his deficiencies for the first time. M. Febvre made this discovery, and has been striving hard for ten years, in the maturity of his career as an actor, to gain an accomplishment possessed by the stripling graduates of the Conservatory. As we are without any such institution here, the rare actors and actresses we have who can freely handle blank-verse must have got their precious gift by nature.

After acting at the various melodramatic theatres, M. Febvre was engaged at the Odéon, and went from there to the Vaudeville, where he played the ardent lover of M. Sardou's " Nos Intimes," known to us as "Friends or Foes," and the preoccupied husband of the eldest daughter of the house in the same author's "Famille Bénoiton," adapted into English as the "Fast Family." From the Vaudeville, M. Febvre passed to the Théâtre Français in 1866, and was made an associate in 1867.

At the Théâtre Français, M. Febvre held an honorable position, but it was not until the production of MM. Erckmann-Chatrian's little three-act play of Alsacian life, "Friend Fritz," that he won a striking victory. This marked triumph was soon succeeded by another, as the American *Clarkson* in M. Dumas's "Étrangère." Each of these parts afforded M. Febvre an opportunity for seizing upon certain external peculiarities of the character, and presenting them forcibly before the eyes of the spectator. Both of the plays were successful; neither of them was of any great value. It may justly be inferred that they owed their run to the strength of the acting. In M. Dumas's "Étrangère" M. Febvre gave a vigorous and vivid portrait of the American, who is the *deus ex machinâ* of that melodramatic comedy, a portrait flattering to American vanity, a portrait of realistic exactness, for which the actor deserves the credit, and not the author. M. Dumas drew a caricature, an impossible American, or rather the impossible American of French stage convention. M. Febvre made this doubtful sketch vital

M. WORMS.

and actual. His *Clarkson* was a man with whom we should not be surprised to meet any day in Chicago or Salt Lake City.

Space fails to give the consideration due to the other actors of the Comédie Française; to M. Maubant, who plays with stately dignity the kings of lordly and loud-sounding tragedy, but whose noble voice, long his chief title to distinction, is beginning to show signs of age; to M. Laroche, a young actor of strength and skill; to M. Thiron, one of the most comic of purely comic actors; and to M. Barré, one of the most amusing of all amusing old men; to M. Ernest Coquelin, the younger brother of the great actor of the same name, hard-working, energetic, full of fantasy and brilliant in farce, and best known as yet for his extraordinarily effective delivery of humorous recitations; or to M. Worms, the fine actor who has recently been admirable beyond peradventure in the part of *Don Carlos* in M. Victor Hugo's "Hernani."

One incident in M. Worms's career needs to be told for the benefit of those who wish to see the theatre subsidized by the state. M. Worms, who is now but little over forty, was graduated from the Conservatory, and entered the Théâtre Français in 1858. In time he made his way, and when, in 1864, there was a vacant share, he was justified in expecting an election as an associate. M. Coquelin was also knocking at the doors for admission, but this did not interfere with M. Worms's expectations. It is not customary for an associate to begin at once with a full share. Both M. Coquelin and M. Worms might be elected, and the share divided between them. This was what they as well as the public generally expected to happen.

But this was during the second Empire, and the actors of the Théâtre Français were called the Comedians in Ordinary of the Emperor. The administration of the imperial theatres was under the supervision of the Ministry of Fine Arts, whose approval was necessary to confirm an election as associate. There was a pretty woman at the Théâtre Français called Mlle. Edile Riquier, who had no special talents except that of being pretty. She had a protector who was high in the imperial favor, and relying on this influence she coveted the half share and the honor of being an associate. In a letter written by the Minister to the manager of the Théâtre Français, Mlle. Riquier's claims were set forth at length, and a plain intimation given that her election would be grateful to the powers that were. In spite of this imperial epistle, the Comédie-Française promptly proceeded to elect unanimously M. Coquelin and M. Worms. The public hoped this would be the end of the scandal, but two weeks later the Minister confirmed M. Coquelin's election and refused to confirm M. Worms, alleging for one thing that he was yet young and could wait, he being at that time twenty-eight, while M. Coquelin was only twenty-two. M. Worms sent in his resignation, and was at once engaged for the French theatre at St. Petersburg, where he remained nearly ten years, returning to France to act in M. Sardou's "Ferréol," and then to be welcomed to the Théâtre Français with open arms. Shortly after M. Worms left Paris for Russia, Mlle. Riquier was arbitrarily made an associate.

Under the Republic which now rules France the Comédie-Française is left to itself, to the great advantage of the stage. If the present government of France move at all in dramatic matters, it will surely be to extend an added honor to the art. Hitherto no actor, while he remained actively on the stage, has been decorated with the cross of the Legion of Honor. This distinction, which has been lavished on every second-rate novelist and dramatist and journalist, even the most eminent actors have died without. It was only bestowed upon M. Regnier after he had definitely retired from the stage. It seems likely now that this survival of mediæval prejudice will die out soon; and the chance of this occurring is none the less for the fact that M. Coquelin is one of the most intimate of M. Gambetta's personal friends.

CHAPTER VIII.

THE THÉÂTRE FRANÇAIS.

DURING every visit I have made to Paris, the performances of the Comédie-Française have been to me a source of unfailing delight. Players might vary in value, now and then an actor might even seem wholly out of place there, and plays might at times be poor and unworthy of acting so fine; but there was always a delightful something in the atmosphere of the House of Molière which suggested that here at least the drama was an art, and that this was its shrine; and which reminded me that here for now two centuries and more the fire lighted by the hand of the master had been watched and tended by faithful guardians.

About the company, the actors and actresses who have succeeded to the places and the parts of Molière and his comrades, much has been written of late—not always profitably, as I fear the readers of the two foregoing chapters will only be too ready to admit. But about the Théâtre Français itself, the actual edifice in which these players play their parts, and within which are imprisoned infinite memories and traditions of the French drama, less is known. To the courtesy of M. Coquelin (to whom I here take pleasure in recording my thanks) I owe the pleasure of a visit to the Théâtre Français and a journey all over it with him as my guide. And I do not know when I have spent time more pleasantly or more profitably than the two hours during which I rambled over the House of Molière

THÉÂTRE FRANÇAIS.

in company with one who plays worthily many of Molière's own parts.

As a theatre merely, the Théâtre Français has been overshadowed of late by the fame of M. Garnier's imperial opera-house; but it is a well-made and good-looking building, as any one can see who takes a glance at the portrait of it which illustrates this chapter. Although it is not as fine or as florid as M. Garnier's Opéra, although it did not spring at once from an architect's brain planned in all its particulars, although it is not even the work of a single architect—it is excellently adapted for its purpose, and is indeed a model of what a theatre should be which is intended for the full enjoyment of acting of an intellectual order, comedy or tragedy. The auditorium is just of the right size for every word to be clearly heard by all: the galleries, which are shallow, contain but a row or two of chairs and a tier of boxes, so that all of the fourteen hundred spectators can see distinctly the slightest play of feature.

The theatre now occupied by the Comédie-Française was opened in 1789 as the theatre of Variétés Amusants. In 1791 a schism had been operated in the Comédie-Française, which was then the tenant of the theatre now called the Odéon, on the other side of the Seine. This schism was caused by the growing, not to say glowing, heat of political feeling. Talma and his republican sympathizers crossed over the river to the Variétés Amusants, and here, after the Directory came in power, the rest of the company were gathered to them. From time to time various improvements have been made in the building. In 1864 the Palais Royal was partly reconstructed, and in the alterations the Théâtre Français gained space for a noble staircase and for the fine *foyer*, or public reception-room, in which the audience may pass the tedious waits. There is now no orchestra at the Théâtre Français to enliven the waits with more or less popular music. There was once, and for a time M. Jacques Offenbach was the leader, but several years ago it was abolished.

It was to find time for needed cleaning and modifications of their theatre, and for the artistic decoration of the auditorium, that the Comédie-Française took its trip to London during the summer of 1879. Much adverse criticism was passed upon the company for crossing the Channel. It was even unkindly hinted that, neglecting the cause of art, the actors and actresses had gone to London to speculate on their reputation and to coin their fame into francs.

Nothing could be less exact. The Comédie-Française had no interest whatever in the receipts of the Gaiety Theatre in London. M. Perrin made an arrangement with the manager of that theatre to cross the Channel, acompanied by the whole Comédie-Française, and to give a series of performances for a fixed sum of six thousand francs a performance. A contract to this effect was made for the express purpose of clearing the reputation of the Comédie-Française from any suggestion of a desire to speculate on its renown. Not only did the actors and actresses of the company undergo the manifold fatigues and discomforts of an exhausting campaign on foreign soil, but they appropriated from their own treasury, for the decoration of the Théâtre Français, a sum in excess of the total amount they were to receive for their services in England. When they returned to Paris, they found their house swept and garnished, and, what was better still, a cordial welcome home at the hands of the Parisians.

Under the arcade of the Rue St. Honoré is the stage door. It is not, like other stage-doors, hid up an alley: it is in the centre of the building and close to the main entrance for the public. A glance at the engraving will show its position; it is under the arcade, about where the carriage stands. It leads to a handsome staircase, where we see the beginning of the large gallery of pictures and statuary belonging to the Comédie-Française, perhaps the finest collection of portraits of dramatic authors and dramatic artists in existence anywhere—a collection indeed so large that it is too much for the space the Comédie can give it, and so it needs must overflow out upon the staircase—where we see the large portrait of Rachel by M. J. L. Gérôme—and upon the passage connecting the stage with the green-room, a passage called the Gallery of Busts, and well lined with marble portraits of many an eminent actor and actress who in the past have honored the history of the Théâtre Français.

Opening off this passage is a room used as a dressing-room by any actor needing to make a hasty change of costume in the course of an act, and not having time to go to his own private room, two or three flights higher up. This little room is hung with portraits of Mademoiselle Clairon as *Medea*, of David Garrick, Mademoiselle Mars, and of Adrienne Lecouvreur. At one end of this passage is the stage, which of necessity is bare of all artistic adornment other than the scenery; and how beautiful this is I need not remind those who have been to this theatre of late, or those who remember that M. Perrin, the manager, is himself a painter, a critic of art, and a pupil of Gros and Delaroche. At one side of the stage is a sort of cabin, comfortably furnished, and used each evening by the actors in the piece while they are not before the audience. The stage itself, M. Coquelin told me, is the best he had ever played on, and so far as he could see it had no faults.

At the other end of the Gallery of Busts is the *foyer* of the artists, or, as we should call it, the green-room. Here are hung the most important of the pictorial treasures of the Comédie—first and foremost the fine portrait of Molière by Mignard, his friend and companion. Then there is a very curious painting, dated 1670, three years before the death of Molière, representing in incongruous medley " the French and Italian farce-actors since sixty years and more;" and here, amid Scaramouche, and Dominique, the harlequin of the Italian comedians, and Gautier Garguille, and Guillot Gorju, and Gros Guillaume, and Jodelet, and other mere fun-makers of the French stage of that day, far over on the left of the picture, stands the great and grave humorist. This painting, which has not yet been engraved, is of great interest; it was discovered almost by accident a few years ago by M. Regnier.

Yet another picture of Moliére is here; it is a wretched little painting by Ingres, given by him to the Comédie, and depicting, years before M. Gérôme attempted the subject, the breakfast which Louis XIV. is said to have offered to Molière—a story which we know now to be without any foundation in fact. And yet, false as the anecdote is, it is generally believed and frequently quoted, and two painters of repute have aided in giving it currency.

It can therefore be scarcely considered a digression to give the facts of the case. In his invaluable volume on the history of the "French Theatre under Louis XIV.," the late Eugène Despois devoted a whole chapter to the demolition of this tale, which he sarcastically entitles the legend of the "en cas de nuit"—the repast always kept ready during night "in case" the king might hunger. As we know, Molière was an hereditary valet-de-chambre of the king, and as such assisted in the formal making of the king's bed. According to the anecdote, some of the noble valets objected to such association with a comedian. To rebuke them, Louis XIV. ordered in the repast that was always in readiness against his royal hunger, and, commanding Molière to sit down, his majesty himself helped him to the wing of a chicken, in the presence of the discomfited courtiers. This is a very pretty story, and it is almost a pity that it is not true. But the evidences in its favor are so slight as to be wellnigh valueless, and the evidence against it is so strong as to be wellnigh overwhelming. In the fierce light which beat upon his throne we see the life of Louis XIV. as we can see that of but few men. Every incident of his long reign is down in black and white in the interminable memoirs and correspondence of the time. But in neither letter nor diary is there any reference to an incident which in the eyes of the courtiers would have been of unexampled importance. The story was first made public in 1823, in the memoirs of Mme. Campan, who said she had it from her father, who had it from an old physician-in-ordinary to Louis XIV. Since 1823 it has been repeated time and again. But there is positive evidence to corroborate the negative. Saint-Simon declares distinctly that, except in the army, the king never ate with any man, not even with the princes of the blood-royal, excepting only at the feasts he gave them at their weddings. In short, the story rests solely upon the second-hand authority of an anonymous physician.

Next in interest to the Molière pictures are two large groups of the company of the Théâtre Français, painted by M. Geffroy, an associate, now retired. In the earlier group, which dates back almost twenty-five years, Mademoiselle Mars and Mademoiselle Rachel are the central figures; and in the later, which is between ten and fifteen years old, Madame Plessy seems to hold the place of honor. Surrounding these pictures, and completely covering on all sides the walls of the room, which is not unduly large, are portraits of many of the greatest of the actors of the past who have been members of the Comédie-Française, beginning with one of Baron, the pupil and friend of Molière, and ending with one of Rachel by M. Dubufe.

Two and three flights of stairs above the greenroom are the dressing-rooms of the actors and actresses. These are not the dingy and dirty little cubby-holes which disgrace many of our theatres. Most of them are good large rooms, with two wide windows opening on the Rue St. Honoré. The one into which I was admitted was hung with antique tapestry and made comfortable by heavy oak furniture, while the walls were adorned with sketches and water-colors by the regretted Henri Regnault, by M. J. G. Vibert, and by M. Madrazo. The work of this last artist was a portrait of M. Coquelin, the

M. COQUELIN AS MASCARILLE (AFTER MADRAZO).

occupant of the dressing-room, as *Mascarille*, one of his best parts.

There is no more reason why an actor or an actress should put up with a mean dressing-room, scant in size and unadorned save with a cheap chair and table, than an artist should do his work in a bare and unsuggestive and unsympathetic studio. The actors and actresses of the Comédie-Française are masters in their own house, and they have given themselves apartments of which an artist has no reason to be ashamed. It would, indeed, be inartistic parsimony for associates of the Comédie-Française, drawing every year no insignificant income from the profits of their labor, if they should slight their own material accommodation while in the Théâtre Français. The share received by the leading actors and actresses for their services during the year 1879 varied from fifty-five thousand francs to seventy thousand. Mlle. Croizette took the former sum, and M. Got the latter. M. Coquelin received sixty-nine thousand, M. Delaunay, sixty-eight thousand, and MM. Febvre, Worms, Thiron, and Maubant each sixty thousand. Mlle. Sarah-Bernhardt had for her share sixty-two thousand, while Mmes. Brohan and Favart had each sixty thousand. A marshal of France gets but thirty thousand francs a year, and an archbishop fifteen thousand—besides, in both cases, incidental allowances and perquisites.

The public *foyer*, in which all visitors to the Théâtre Français have doubtless passed one or more quarters of an hour seeking relief, during the long tedious waits between the acts, from the heat and the closeness caused by the insufficient ventilation of the theatre—as insufficient even here as in the other theatres of Paris—has nearly as many works of art as the green-room, but they are statuary, not paintings. The square lobby, and the long and narrow gallery which runs out from it, along the Rue de Richelieu, are lined with busts of famous French dramatists. In the lobby are vigorous heads of Corneille and Rotrou by Caffieri.

There also are two of the best works of Houdon—the bust of Molière and the remarkably life-like seated statue of Voltaire. At the end of the gallery, after passing a dozen busts of very varying merit, but including one of Jean Jacques Rousseau, by Caffieri, is a sitting statue of George Sand, the only woman, with the exception of Madame de Girardin, it may be mentioned, who has ever held a foremost place among the dramatists of France. And not only the lobby and the gallery, but all the approaches to it—the handsome staircase which rises from the Rue St. Honoré, the vestibules and waiting-rooms—all are decorated with statues and busts. On the ground floor, just by a flight of stairs, is a striking head of the elder Dumas, the negro blood fully apparent in the thick lips and flattened nose of this most fertile of all French novelists.

In the brilliant preface (not long published) to his latest play, the "Étrangère," acted with popular approval at this theatre, the younger M. Dumas looks into the future, wondering whether anything of his may survive the attack of time. One passage calls for quotation here:

"Those who, like myself, have had some few pieces represented on the stage of the Théâtre Français have rather more chance than the others —even when their comedies are no longer played— of being occasionally spoken of, because of the marble busts of them which the committee can, if it likes, place on the stairway, the lobby, or the vestibules. If that honor is ever accorded me, they will probably place the bust which Carpeaux made of me opposite the bust which Chapu made of my father, at the foot of the grand staircase. We shall then look on, without seeing them, at all the beauties who pass into the play, and when they come down, after the performance, perhaps one of them, while she awaits her carriage, will cast a nonchalant glance upon the marble image, and will say something—no matter what—about the man and his work. Thanks, madam, thanks in advance; one could scarcely hope for more, and, as for myself, that little corner immortality would completely satisfy me."

At the side of the main entrance are seated statues of Mademoiselle Mars as "Comedy" and Mademoiselle Rachel as "Tragedy."

Since my visit to the Théâtre Français, M. Réné Delorme has published "The Museum of the Comédie-Française," an ample volume of over two hundred quarto pages, in which the riches of Molière's house are set forth in order, exactly, and with fulness. Hereafter a visitor to the Théâtre Français need not rely wholly on the word-of-mouth catalogue of his courteous conductors, for here in print is a seemingly complete list of the treasures of the building. M. Delorme points out that this museum (for such is the theatre in reality) is but little known, even to Parisians, for want perhaps of a list of its contents; and this in spite of the fact that it contains pictures by Mignard, Van Loo, David, Gros, Ingres, Delacroix, Isabey, Dubufe, Gérôme, and Robert-Fleury, and statues by Houdon, Caffieri, Dantan, Clésinger, and David d'Angers.

The museum is about a hundred years old, and M. Delorme gives us a history of its growth. In 1777, when the company owned a picture or two, Caffieri proposed to found a gallery of great French dramatists and actors, to which he himself made the first contributions. In 1815 there were a dozen paintings and nearly two dozen marbles. In 1850 M. Arsène Houssaye became the director, and his artistic taste gave great impulse to the collection, which has continued to grow under the present director, M. Émile Pérrin. The total catalogue of works of art now belonging to the Comédie-Française reckons over three hundred numbers, including one hundred and seventy-one pictures and seventy-seven marbles.

Away up in the fourth story, high over the public lobby and its gallery, along the Rue de Richelieu, are the archives and the library. Here in long and narrow apartments, lighted by frequent windows overlooking the Place du Théâtre Français, are freely opened the invaluable records of the theatre which was founded over two hundred years ago by the greatest of French dramatists, and which in its two centuries of existence has produced fresh from the author's pen the best works of the best of his successors—precious manuscripts from the hands of most of whom are here jealously hoarded.

Here is the series of registers for each year—registers in which is noted day by day every incident of the history of the Comédie; the reading and reception of every new play; its cast; its success when produced; the nightly receipts; and the transient indisposition of any performer. This long line of registers begins with that more precious than any, written in his own hand, by Charles Varlet de La Grange, the fellow-actor of Molière, his successor in the post of *orateur*, or spokesman of the company, during the great humorist's life, and after his death the real head of the company he left behind him. There are no breaks in this succession of annual records, save that the volume for 1740 has been lost, and that caused by the dispersion of the Comédie-Française in 1793; it was no time then to act or register acting. In the words of the old Mazarinade,

> Comédiens, c'est mauvais temps,
> La Tragédie est par les champs.

Owing to this dispersion the archives of the Comédie Française were in a sorry state of confusion; books and papers of all kinds were heaped together on the floor in closets, wholly without order.

It is only within the last twenty-five years, and since the appointment of the late Léon Guillard as archivist and librarian, that the records have been arranged. And when they were finally set in order, many a treasure was discovered amongst them— autographs, letters, manuscripts of all kinds, of authors, of actors and actresses, of courtiers, critics, and literary people of all grades. There is, for instance, a holograph manuscript of the "Marriage of Figaro," which, with many another document here preserved and thus recently brought to light, has been utilized by MM. d'Heylli and Marescot in their excellent four-volume edition of Beaumarchais's plays. The library owes its existence for the most part to M. Guillard, who began to gather theatrical books of all classes—memoirs, criticisms, editions of dramatists, etc. The collection is only promising as yet, and not to be compared with the ample body of books which M. Nuitter has got together at the Opéra. Both collections, it is a pleasure to add, are readily thrown open to any visitor who comes properly introduced.

After the death of M. Guillard, M. François Coppée, the poet, and the author of the lovely " Violin-maker of Cremona," acted at this theatre, was appointed archivist; and the onerous post of librarian was given to M. Monval, an erudite in the past of the French drama, and the author of a history of the Odéon Theatre. Before taking leave of the archives which he guards with such cheerful courtesy, let me quote one of the many autographs which in frames line the walls of the library where these are not covered with books. It is the epitaph on Molière written by the hand of Lafontaine, and signed as you see:

Sur Moliere.

Sous ce tombeau gisent Plaute et Terence,
Et cependant le seul Moliere y gist,
Leurs trois talens ne formoient qu'un esprit
Dont le bel art rejouissoit la france.
Ils sont partis ! et j'ay peu d'espérance
De les revoir. Malgré tous nos efforts
Pour un long temps, selon toute apparence,
Térence, et Plaute, et Moliere sont morts.
DELAFONTAINE.

CHAPTER IX.

THE OTHER COMEDY THEATRES.

THE early history of the Parisian stage is filled with the recital of the wars waged by the three royal and privileged theatres against their unauthorized rivals. The story is very like that of the strife of the patent theatres in London against their intermittent competitors. In Paris the three privileged theatres were the Opéra, the Comédie-Française, and the Italian Comedy (which afterward became the Opéra Comique). They claimed that a royal patent conferred exclusive rights; but the advocates of liberty were finally successful, and in 1795 there were fifty-one theatres open at once in Paris. In 1807 Napoleon suppressed all but eight, and rigidly restricted each of the survivors to a special style of performance. This forbade anything like rivalry, and from want of healthy competition stagnation would have resulted, if the decree had not been partly abrogated upon the Restoration. In 1867 it was totally abolished; and since then the number of theatres in Paris and its suburbs has rapidly grown. There are now not far from fifty places of amusement which one may fairly enough call theatres.

It will be obviously impossible to consider all these establishments in detail; the more important must be selected for description. For the purpose of critical examination, the theatres of Paris—excluding the various opera-houses already fully treated, and the Théâtre Français—may be roughly divided into three broad classes. First, those devoting themselves especially to comedy, and in a measure saying ditto to the Théâtre Français. Second, those of ampler size and appealing to large audiences, with the alternating attractions of melodrama and spectacle. And thirdly, the houses of entertainment of an altogether lighter and brighter class, enticing the passer-by with farce and extravaganza, with vaudeville and opéra bouffe, with parodies and pieces of pleasantry of all kinds.

In the first class are to be included the Odéon, or Second Théâtre Français, the Gymnase Dramatique, the Vaudeville, and perhaps a more distant and less important house which now calls itself the Third Théâtre Français. It is this class of theatre which, in some respects, is the most interesting to the American inquirer, because it is only with these that any comparison can fairly be made with the best of our American theatres.

It must be remembered that when we speak of the superiority of the French stage to our own—a superiority which it would be futile to deny—what is meant is not that all the acting in Paris is good, or that all the acting in New York is bad. There are probably now not only as good actors, but as many good actors in the United States as in France. And as Mr. Lewes wrote in 1865, "there is abundance of bad acting to be seen in Paris as elsewhere."

The remark is as true now as it was fifteen years ago. Many of the secondary companies in Paris are but little, if any, better than companies of corresponding position here. I certainly have seen one performance in Paris as bad as any I ever saw in New York. And the provincial theatres of France are said to be in a deplorable state. It has been pointed out that, owing to the centralization, which is the great curse of France, the capital monopolizes the best actors, and gathers them into a few—a very few indeed—strong and select stock companies. The stranger, seeing that these few theatres in Paris give finer and fuller performances of comedy than any theatre in London or New York, not unnaturally infers that the whole stage of France is just so much better than the whole stage of England or America.

Theatrically speaking, Paris is France; but New York is not the United States. I doubt whether there are better actors in France than the United States, although Paris presents many more than New York. I doubt whether there are any actors in France who, in their respective lines, are more richly gifted or better trained than Mr. Joseph Jefferson, or Mr. Lester Wallack, or Mr. W. J. Florence, or Mr. J. H. Stoddart; although, on the other hand, we have no M. Got, no M. Coquelin, no M. Delaunay. But M. Got and M. Coquelin and M. Delaunay are all in one theatre, and at times are cast in one play, and have for years been in the habit of playing together; while Mr. Florence and Mr. Jefferson and Mr. Stoddart often play a thousand miles apart.

The French are not cursed with the "star" system; they will not tolerate a single planet set in a fading cloud of star-dust. And thus centralization and the habit of having stock companies combine to help Paris to good playing, while the broad extent and well-diffused wealth of our land unite with the star system to prevent good players from massing together here in New York. This, and not any lack of good actors, is the reason why we have here no theatre equal to the Gymnase or the Vaudeville, not to mention the Comédie-Française.

It would doubtless be difficult, even if possessed of autocratic power, to gather from all the United States a company better than the Comédie-Française—better, that is, than the male half of that admirable assemblage of picked comedians; the female half, as we have seen, in spite of several personalities of strange and pungent flavor, is not at all on the same artistic level. It would certainly be impossible, in the United States, to compose, off-hand and at once, a company which should immediately begin to work together as smoothly as the traditions and restraints of two hundred years of existence enabled the comedians of the Théâtre Français to work. But from the theatres of New York, from out of the stock companies of this one

ODÉON.

city, could readily be chosen a company which, after it should have time to get into working order, would compare not unfavorably with that of the Odéon, or of the Vaudeville, or of the Gymnase.

The Odéon theatre was built under Louis XVI., and was occupied for a while by the Comédie-Française. It is one of the largest houses in

The Other Comedy Theatres. 159

Paris, containing seventeen hundred places. It has the distinction of having been the first theatre in which those admitted to the pit were provided with seats. The "Marriage of Figaro," the forerunner of the Revolution, was originally acted at the Odéon. In 1799 the theatre was burned, and the Comédie-Française crossed the river again to the Palais Royal. Rebuilt, it was called the Theatre of the Empress. Two incidents of its early career are of interest to Americans: at different times two French plays on the career of the Father of his Country, were acted within its walls. July 13th, 1791, two years before the reign of terror, saw the first performance of "Washington; or, Liberty in the New World," a drama in four acts, by Sauvigny, one of the Royal Censors. January 5th, 1813, two years before the battle of Waterloo, witnessed the production of "Washington; or, Retaliation," a drama in three acts, by Henri Lacoste. This last, we are told by the historian of the Odéon, M. Monval, now the librarian of the Théâtre Français, but at one time an actor at the Odéon, was a great success.

In 1818 the theatre was burnt again, but at once rebuilt by the order of Louis XVIII., who gave it permission to act all the plays of the classic repertory, hitherto the exclusive right of the Comédie-Française. It was at this time that the Odéon became the second Théâtre Français, a title which it retains to the present day. It keeps a certain number of classic comedies and tragedies constantly in readiness, in return for which and for bringing out the plays of young authors, it receives an annual subsidy from the state. Without this governmental aid it would barely be able to exist, for its situation is unfortunate, and in spite of a long list of brilliant successes, its history is for the most part a record of failures. It is the centre of the students' quarter, and they are rather hard customers to please. It was here that M. Victorien Sardou's first play was acted; it was a comedy in verse called the " Student's Tavern ; " and it was damned out of hand.

In general the use of the Odéon has been to feed the Théatre Français with plays and players. Many of the best modern pieces in the repertory of the Théâtre Français have been borrowed from the Odéon. Many of the important actors and actresses now at the Comédie-Française have come to it from the Odéon.

It was at the Odéon that Casimir Delvigne made his first great hit with the " Sicilian Vespers; " that Ponsard made his with " Lucrèce ; " that M. Émile Augier made his with the lovely little comedy of classic life, the " Ciguë " (the " Hemlock "); and that George Sand made hers with the " Marquis of Villemer." The latest long run which has taken place within its walls is the " Danicheffs,"

The Other Comedy Theatres. 161

written by a Russian gentleman, and revised, if not remade entirely, by M. Dumas.

The Vaudeville Theatre was founded in 1792 by two writers of light musical pieces, who had quarrelled with Sédaine, then the manager of the Opéra Comique. As its name declared, it was to

VAUDEVILLE.

be devoted to vaudevilles. In the original sense of the word, a vaudeville was a sort of occasional epigram. Throughout the seventeenth century it was the name given to the numberless personal and political ballads of the period, not wanting in salt and satire. In time the name got transferred to little plays all in song. These in turn grew in importance. At last in our own century the word came to have a definite dramatic meaning. A vaudeville is now a play, in any number of acts from one to five, on any sort of subject (although it is almost always light and amusing), but with this one peculiarity—that at intervals throughout the piece, songs are sung to well-known airs. In its simplest form the vaudeville is a little one-act play, the best points of the dialogue of which the author has polished into epigrams sung to the most familiar and often old-fashioned airs. With the growth of opéra bouffe the vaudeville has declined; and although its influence is still marked on the minor dramatic literature of France, there is no longer in Paris any theatre set apart specially for this purely French form of entertainment.

Even at the Vaudeville Theatre itself, it is now a very rare thing to hear a vaudeville. For fifty years the Vaudeville was true to its first love, in the beginning with good fortune, in the end with unmitigated ill-luck. But in 1852 there was brought out at the Vaudeville a play, by the son of the great Dumas, containing, of course, the one song which the authorities required at this theatre during the reign of the principle of confining each house to its special department of the drama. This play was the "Dame aux Camélias," known to us as "Camille." Of its success it is unnecessary to speak. It was followed by the late Théodore Barrière's " Filles de Marbre," popular even now on the American stage as the " Marble Heart." These two plays (the latter intended as an antidote to the former) have suffered grievously in process of preparing them for the American market. Fortunately the time has now come when we get our dramatic goods in the original package, and can judge of their merits for ourselves.

The new vein of rich ore which the Vaudeville had struck, by accident as it were, it has continued to work ever since with varying fortune, for the most part favorable. In time came the " Romance of a Poor Young Man," of M. Octave Feuillet, then writing in his earlier and sentimental manner. A few years later, M. Sardou saw his " Bénoiton Family " make a hit which he has never since been able to equal.

In 1869 the march of municipal improvement found the Vaudeville in its path. It was situated then opposite the Bourse, the Parisian stock-exchange. Forced to move, the city authorities built for it a handsome theatre, in a very advantageous position in the Boulevard des Italiens. It had scarcely got settled before the troubles of foreign and intestine war came upon Paris, and broke up all chance of profit. After the war, it took some time for it to get on its feet again. Then came the long run of " Pink Dominoes." Not long after, in

1877, M. Sardou, who had given it two political plays, "Rabagas" and "Uncle Sam," of questionable success and of unquestionable bad taste, wrote for it one of his finest and firmest works, "Dora," which we know in America in the Anglified adaptation called "Diplomacy."

The Gymnase Dramatique is barely threescore years old, having been opened in 1820, as a sort of public practice-room for the graduates of the Conservatory. From the beginning the Gymnase relied upon the fertile pen of Eugène Scribe, who wrote for it in the first ten years of its career fully one hundred and fifty plays—most of them, it is true, in one act only. It is scarcely too much to say that the Gymnase was created by Scribe, and sustained by him, aided by the army of collaborators to whom he subsequently dedicated his collected works.

Bayard's "Fils de Famille" (known in America as "The Lancers") was one of the early successes of the Gymnase. Its main dependence was for years upon M. Sardou, M. Barrière, and the younger M. Dumas. Although it was at the Vaudeville that M. Dumas gained his first victory with the "Dame aux Camélias" (splendidly played by Fechter and Madame Doche), he was, until a short time ago, bound by treaty to write only for the Gymnase. His "Monsieur Alphonse" was at one time running there contemporaneously with M. Sardou's "Uncle

Sam" at the Vaudeville, and M. Dumas declared that his piece was better than M. Sardou's, for he could not sit out "Uncle Sam," and he had seven times patiently listened to " M. Alphonse."

M. Dumas was fortunate in finding at the Gymnase two such consummate actresses as Mme. Rose Chéri, who created the chief part in his "Demi-Monde," and Mlle. Desclée, who lent to the "Princess Georges" the aid of her extraordinary ability.

It was at the Gymnase M. Sardou brought out his "Pattes de Mouche," only recently acted here in New York as the "Scrap of Paper." At the Gymnase were also acted M. Sardou's "Fernande," and "Séraphine," and "Ferréol." And it was at the Gymnase that Mlle. Desclée gave a truthful portrait of the wayward heroine of MM. Meilhac and Halévy's most Parisian comedy "Frou-frou," so touchingly acted in this country by Miss Agnes Ethel. Of late the Gymnase has not been in luck. From being a theatre in which nearly everything pleased the popular taste, it has become a theatre where an extended list of failures is broken now and again by a complete triumph.

Most of the theatres of Paris keep up the old custom of prefixing a one-act play to the important play which forms the staple of the evening's entertainment. It is a great pity that this is no longer the fashion in this country; and it is to be hoped that the custom will not fall into disuse in Paris.

It affords a young author an opportunity for presenting himself to the public, and of trying his wings, so to speak, before attempting a loftier flight. The manager who might well hesitate to produce an important play by a promising beginner can readily afford to risk a little one-act comedy, the failure of which is no great matter.

An amusing anecdote is told of one aspiring but stuttering dramatist, who, after many attempts, was able at last to get a manager to listen to his little play. When the author, whose nervousness had increased his impediment, had finished reading his act, the manager delighted him with the assurance that the play was accepted and would be done speedily. He was pleased with it, he added, because the idea was so new; there had never before been a play in which all the characters stammered.

"B-b-but," hesitated the young dramatist, "it is I th-th-that s-stutter, and n-n-not the c-c-characters!"

Whereupon the manager abruptly answered, "Then I don't care for the piece! Good morning!"

CHAPTER X.

THE THEATRES OF DRAMA AND SPECTACLE.

THERE are five important theatres devoted to drama and spectacular pieces—the Porte St. Martin, a simple but dignified building, on the site of the old house destroyed during the disturbances of the Commune; the Châtelet, badly injured at the same time, but now convalescent; the Ambigu-Comique, once unlucky but now returning to favor; the Lyrique, intended for a popular opera-house, but at present called the Théâtre des Nations; and the Chateau d'Eau. A sixth house, the Gaîté, belongs under this head, although for the moment it is devoted to operatic performances.

Nearly all the buildings are comparatively modern, yet three of the establishments date back into the last century. The Porte St. Martin was opened in 1781, the Gaîté in 1772, and the Ambigu-Comique in 1769. The Porte St. Martin was the theatre which the architect Lenoir built in ninety odd days for the Opéra, and which, as I have told in an earlier chapter, the profane throng were allowed to test before sacred royalty ventured in. The Gaîté and the Ambigu-Comique at first were but little more than booths in which various shows were exhibited—gymnastics, acrobatics, rope-walking, juggling, feats of skill, and feats of strength, marionettes, and so forth—all, no doubt to the great amusement of the good people of Paris, as well as of the noble courtiers who also came to see the sights. The Gaîté was at first called the "Theatre of the King's Great Dancers." Rarce-shows of all sorts helped to make up

> "The little great, the infinite small thing
> That ruled the hour when Louis Quinze was king.
>
> "For these were yet the days of halcyon weather,
>   A Martin's summer, when the nation swam
> Aimless and easy as a wayward feather,
>   Down the full tide of jest and epigram;
> A careless time, when France's bluest blood
> Beat to the tune of 'After us the flood.'"

At last the floods came and beat upon that royal house, and swept it away into outer darkness. And of the new-found liberty the theatres had their full share. They gave up the acrobatic for the melodramatic, and juggled with the emotions instead of three gilt balls. While they were seeking a new method of stirring the human heart some dim echo of the German storm-and-stress outbreak seems to have come from the frontier. The multitudinous and well-made German melodrama was speedily naturalized in France, then ready to greet any stranger as a citizen. The new style was improved by French skill, and it met at once with popular acceptance. The field was all the fairer for these larger houses appealing to the broader public, from the fact that the leading literary theatres remained in bondage to the theories of Voltaire and his weakening successors. Indeed, as will be shown, the romantic revival was to be wrought rather in the melodramatic houses than in the classic theatres.

PORTE ST. MARTIN.

In 1802 the Porte St. Martin, which had not been regularly occupied since the Opéra emigrated from it eight years before, was opened with a melodrama in three acts, called "Pizarro; or, the Conquest of Peru." This drama, acted in Paris, was doubtless derived from the same play of Kotzebue's from which Sheridan had taken the " Pizarro " in which he had written for *Rolla* the patriotic harangue against the foreign invader that every visitor to Drury Lane Theatre applied to the French foemen only across the Channel.

Like most of the minor theatres, the Porte St. Martin was closed in 1807. It was opened again in 1810. One of the attractions it offered in this latter year was " The Passage of Mount St. Bernard " by Napoleon and his army, a spectacle which the great commander deigned to honor with his presence.

After the Restoration, the Porte St. Martin devoted itself to melodrama, enlivening its playbill with an occasional spectacular fairy piece. Its greatest success was with " Thirty Years ; or, a Gambler's Life," in which Frédérick Lemaître and Mme. Dorval divided the triumph. During the end of the Bourbon rule there was rebellion on foot in literature as well as in politics. There was a stern determination to throw off the yoke of the so-called unities.

In all the furious fighting between the young blood, which was called Romantic, and the old school, which called itself Classic, the Porte St. Martin bore its share; and its stage was the scene of many a pitched battle. On it were first performed the " Marino Faliero " of Casimir Delavigne, the " Tour de Nesle " and " Antony " of Alexandre

Dumas the elder, and the "Marie Tudor" and "Lucrèce Borgia" of Victor Hugo. "Lucrèce Borgia," curtailed to libretto size, is familiar to all. The "Tour de Nesle" has been played in every language in every quarter of the globe. "'Antony,'" said Dumas, "and my son are my two best works."

Victor Hugo and Dumas were not alone; they were surrounded by a score of young writers—Vacquerie, Meurice, Pyat, Gérard de Nerval—who copied the force as well as the faults of their masters. They added the skill of born dramatists to the instinct of trained playwrights. They understood that the backbone of every good drama should be action; that the secret of theatrical success, in three words, is action, action, action! Reviving the vogue of the Spanish dramas of cloak and sword, they touched the hearts of the myriad-headed, myriad-handed theatrical public, while they fitted with parts and brought into notice a host of excellent actors—four of whom deserve especial record, Frédérick Lemaître, Bocage, Mlle. Georges, and Mme. Dorval.

"When I think," says Thackeray in that Paris Sketch-Book which Mr. Michael Angelo Titmarsh dedicated to his tailor, " over the number of crimes that I have seen Mademoiselle Georges commit, I am filled with wonder at her greatness, and the greatness of the poets who have conceived these charming horrors for her. I have seen her make love to and murder her sons in the ' Tour de Nesle.' I have seen her poison a company of no less than nine gentlemen, at Ferrara, with an affectionate son in the number; I have seen her as *Madame de Brinvilliers* kill off numbers of respectable relations in the first four acts; and, at the last, be actually burned at the stake, to which she comes shuddering, ghastly, and in a white sheet. Sweet excitement of tender sympathies! Such tragedies are not so good as a real, downright execution, but, in point of interest, the next thing to it; with what a number of moral emotions do they fill the breast; with what a hatred for vice, and yet a true pity and respect for that grain of virtue that is to be found in us all: our bloody, daughter-loving *Brinvilliers;* our warm-hearted, poisonous *Lucrezia Borgia;* above all, what a smart appetite for a cool supper afterwards, at the Café Anglais, when the horrors of the play act as a piquant sauce to the supper!'"

Perhaps the greatest of the four great artists of the romantic period of the French drama, Frédérick Lemaître, long survived Bocage, Mlle. Georges, and Mme. Dorval. After playing in "Thirty Years; or, a Gambler's Life," with Mme. Dorval, he created—and here the use of the French idiom is exact—"Robert Macaire," transmuting the cheap melodrama into a colossal caricature almost Aristophanic in its grandiose buffoonery. Perfected by the wit of Philipon and the pencil of Daumier, "Robert Macaire" has remained a type. In 1835, after playing *Gennaro* in "Lucrèce Borgia," and *Richard Darlington*, Frédérick Lemaître visited England, where he was well received. It can hardly be doubted that his powerful but occasionally vulgar acting exerted a visible influence upon Dickens (then only beginning to be known as "Boz"), with whose nature his had much in common.

Upon his return to France, Frédérick Lemaître appeared in "Kean," a piece of tawdry bombast, by the elder Dumas, unworthy of criticism, but effectively contrived to show off the varied genius of the actor. To Edmund Kean, from whom the play borrowed only its name, the French critics frequently likened him. Gautier called him "the only actor who reminds us of Garrick, Kemble, Macready, and especially Kean"—a conjunction of names which must appear absurd to any one who knows the unlikeness to each other of the actors thus grouped together. Mr. Lewes says that to "speak of Lemaître as a rival of Kean or Rachel seems to me like comparing Eugène Sue with Victor Hugo—the gulf that separates prose from poetry yawns between them." M. Hugo himself thought otherwise; in the note appended to "Ruy Blas," in which Lemaître acted the hero, the author declares that "for the old he is Lekain and Garrick in one; for us he has the action of Kean united to the emotion of Talma." He was often called "the Talma of the boulevards."

It is related that at the first reading of "Ruy Blas" Lemaître supposed that he was to play, not the hero, but *Don César de Bazan*, an incident which perhaps suggested to that skilful playwright, M. Dennery, the setting of *Don César* in a separate play, of which Lemaître should be the protagonist. After this, his next important part was the *Chiffonier* of M. Félix Pyat, the socialist dramatist, who saw scenes even more bloody in real life than he had ever thought to put on the stage. In Balzac's "Vautrin," his make-up to resemble Louis Philippe caused the suppression of the play. Mr. Lewes, whose temperate opinion seems more just than the enthusiastic eulogies of the French, thought Frédérick Lemaître "singularly gifted" and of "exceptional genius," but he detected in him "something offensive to good taste," "a note of vulgarity, partly owing to his daring animal spirits, but mainly owing, I suspect, to an innate vulgarity of nature."

The romantic revival spent itself at last, and the mantle of Delavigne and Dumas fell on MM. Dennery, Dumanoir, and Dugué; drama descended to melodrama; heroics were succeeded by cheap sentiment; the once fertile field became a desert. Occasionally there appeared an oasis, like the "Patrie" of M. Sardou; but the broad plain remained an arid waste. Authors and managers tried to attract by heaping together horrors—adultery, rape, incest, murder, and suicide—all in one play. For a time they succeeded; the interest of the jaded public was aroused, but the accumulation of atrocities has its limits, and, when author and manager had gone to the end of their tether, the public again abandoned them, deserting to the hostile camp of opéra bouffe. For years drama had a hard struggle for existence, but to-day, satiated with the champagne of opéra bouffe, the fickle affection of the Parisian play-goers is again given to the Porte St. Martin and its rivals.

That the Parisian public should like gaudy shows is, in part at least, the fault of former managers of the Porte St. Martin, the Gaîté, and the other houses legitimately devoted to the bolder forms of the drama, inasmuch as they had accustomed the play-goers of France to spectacular profusion in a quick succession of gorgeous fairy plays, rivalling one another in emptiness and meretricious glare. One of these show-pieces acted at the Porte St. Martin was imported to New York as the "White Fawn." During the run of this play at the time of the Exhibition of 1867, for a fortnight or so, Mademoiselle Sarah-Bernhardt acted the part of the princess.

After the war and the two sieges of Paris, it might be supposed that a more worthy form of entertainment would be proffered. But at the Gaîté there was very soon seen a fairy piece called "King Carrot," written by M. Victorien Sardou, with music composed by M. Jacques Offenbach, and produced with the same glitter and show. Not long after, a patriotic play by M. Barbier, on "Joan of Arc," had a memorable career at the same theatre, for which, no doubt, it was indebted to the noble music contributed by M. Charles Gounod. The theatre again lapsed into sensational shows, hybrid compounds of acting and singing and dancing and personal exhibition. The two most notorious of these spectacles were revised editions of M. Offenbach's "Orphée aux Enfers" and "Génévieve of Brabant."

The Porte St. Martin Theatre, burnt to the ground as the Communists gave up their government, was rebuilt, and in 1873 it reopened with the "Marie Tudor" of M. Victor Hugo. It happens that the first poets of our time in England and in France have chosen ill-fated Queen Mary as the heroine of a play, and nothing can well be more characteristic of the two nationalities, than a comparison of the French play with the English. Both lyrists, as it happens, have no mean opinion of themselves. To flatter the innocent vanity of the author of "Marie Tudor," the managers of the Porte St. Martin were guilty of a little deception.

The story runs—as to its truth I will not commit myself—that every afternoon when M. Victor Hugo left the stage door of the theatre, after the rehearsal of "Marie Tudor," he found half a hundred of the populace waiting for his coming, and greeting him on his appearance with hearty and prolonged cheers and cries of "Vive Victor Hugo!" To which the poet, as in duty bound, responded with a courtly bow. But M. Hugo, although vain, is not blind. The regularity, not to say monotony, of this afternoon enthusiasm was suspicious, and at last the poet began to suspect. One day the two managers of the theatre walked out with him after the rehearsal, and as soon as the group in the street saw the dramatist, the regular excitement was exhibited, and the air was rent as usual with cheers and cries of " Vive Victor Hugo!" The poet turned to the senior manager and with a keen smile said quietly :

"You keep your supers in good training!"

The next time M. Victor Hugo left the theatre there was no fictitious populace to greet him with manufactured enthusiasm. But in spite all the skill of the managers, the revival of "Marie Tudor" did not attract the public. Nor did the ensuing dramas, until, in January, 1874, the "Two Orphans" came to fill the theatre to repletion, and the treasury to the satisfaction of authors and directors.

With the following piece the Porte St. Martin gave us the first specimen of a new kind of play.

By dint of extravagance and stupidity, the old fairy plays, on the gayety and lightness of which the former managers had relied to contrast now and then with the serious sombreness of their ordinary dramas, had at last wholly worn themselves out, and lost the favor of the public. So a new type of piece came into being, and, according to the spirit of the age, it was scientific—at least in its pretensions. M. Jules Verne had been writing pseudo-scientific tales of adventure for a decade, and out of one of these the unerring hand of M. Dennery fashioned a play in which a continued dramatic interest was combined with boundless opportunities of spectacular display.

"The Trip Around the World in Eighty Days" proved, by its long lease of life on the boards of the Porte St. Martin, that the public were pleased with plays of this new kind; and within the past five years half-a-dozen others on the same model have been brought out. All of these lack the freshness of the first. All of them, like the first, are more or less geographic. M. Bélot's " Black Venus," acted at the Châtelet, was a drama of African exploration—surely as sterile a subject of dramatic treatment as one could well discover. It was the old show piece over again, only, if possible, a little duller. Troops of strange animals were brought from the menageries to tramp across the stage night after night. Between the acts a drop curtain is lowered, on which is painted a huge map of Africa, with the route of the heroes of the piece distinctly marked. One might as well go to a meeting of the Geographical Society at once, as expect true dramatic entertainment from any such

CHÂTELET.

theatrical slicing and serving up of a traveller's itinerary.

The present tendency of the theatres of this class is apparently toward military pieces, fife and drum chronicles, full of sound and fury, crammed with patriotism and buncombe, and signifying very little indeed. The military piece is another attempt to combine dramatic interest with spectacular display, an attempt which a large popular theatre, having to appeal to the eyes as well as the ears of its customer, is always making, but rarely with the result expected.

Since the extended run of the "Two Orphans" at the Porte St. Martin theatre, the latest play which has aimed at purely dramatic effects, and which has been granted long life, is the dramatization of M. Zola's naturalistic novel, the "Assommoir," performed at the Ambigu-Comique. The piece was acted nearly three hundred times, and its first performance excited as much attention as the first appearance of the striking and powerful story from which it was taken. Indeed its production was a solemnity which has been likened to the bringing out of M. Victor Hugo's "Hernani," half a century before. Like M. Hugo, M. Zola has a theory of dramatic art which he has set forth in his theatrical criticisms in the *Bien Public* and the *Voltaire*. They may be roughly summarized by saying that he wants to see the same realism on the stage which he has already applied to the novel.

M. Zola had three times put this to the proof by appearing as a dramatic author, and as many times failed. He did not dramatize his own novel; this was done by two expert theatrical hacks. M. Sarcey in the *Temps* said that the piece raised no literary questions, and was very easy to judge; it was simply one of those plays of which the sole criticism needed is to record whether it pleased or bored the public; it had no higher views. " The name of M. Zola and his noisily-paraded pretentions of creating a new theory of theatrical art ought not to delude us. The 'Assommoir' will regenerate nothing; it is a play like many we have seen, and shall see again." M. Sarcey then pointed out that the first half of the piece is light and gay, and that the final scenes are monotonous and wearisome when they are not revolting.

M. Zola not long since published in a single volume the three plays written by himself which were summarily damned when acted, accompanying each with a preface in which he explains what his intentions were in writing it, and expresses his surprise that they were not more readily recognized. In spite of failure, M. Zola is not discouraged; he believes in his theories and he has faith in himself. The final paragraph of his preface to this volume of dramas contains these characteristic words:

" I publish my hissed plays, and I wait. They are three — the three first soldiers of an army. When there are twenty they will make themselves respected. What I wait for is an evolution in our dramatic literature, a change of the public and of the critics in their attitude toward me, a clearer and juster appreciation of what I am and of what I mean. They have ended at last by reading my novels; they will end by hearing my plays."

CHAPTER XI.

THE THEATRES OF FARCE AND EXTRAVAGANZA.

THE houses of comic entertainment in Paris are, in some respects, the most characteristic production of French civilization. There are in Paris six or seven theatres devoted to farce and extravaganza, to vaudeville and opéra bouffe. At first opéra bouffe was but little more than an ambitious vaudeville. Suddenly it started into luxuriant life under the magic wand of Herr Offenbach. Beginning with the " Deux Aveugles " at the tiny Folies-Marigny, in the Champs Elysées, it gained the Bouffes-Parisiens, where the energetic composer-manager produced " Orphée aux Enfers," in which for a few nights only the notorious Cora Pearl as *Cupid* exhibited herself, her diamonds, and her incompetence.

Then it spread to the Variétés, took firm root and blossomed into that brilliant series of satires beginning with the " Belle Hélène," and including the " Grand Duchess of Gérolstein." Ungrateful opéra bouffe almost killed its elder brother the vaudeville, and in 1867, when at the height of its power, it threatened to kill melodrama. But the managers of the larger theatres fought the foe with his own weapons ; it had been drama against vaudeville; it should be spectacle against opéra bouffe.

The war of 1870 did wonders. It did not kill opéra bouffe. The success of the "Timbale d'Argent," and of a few of its followers, is too great to allow us to think that; but a demand was awakened for something different. It is perhaps safer to say that the rage for opéra bouffe having passed away, that production resolved itself into its original elements. Opéra bouffe was a compound of comic opera and of comic drama. With the disappearance of opéra bouffe comes the reappearance in great force of comic opera and of comic drama; and a classification of these minor theatres is now possible.

The Bouffes-Parisiens is almost the only theatre which has remained true to its old love. It has as a competitor just now only the Fantaisies. The Renaissance and the Folies-Dramatiques have already been described in the chapter on the minor music theatres; they have developed opéra bouffe into what is very like the old and early form of opéra comique. The Variétés and the Palais Royal have returned to the comic drama of a broadly farcical type, with only occasional and subordinate music; and the Athenée and Théâtre des Arts follow their lead. A ninth and new theatre, the Nouveautés, opened in the Boulevard during the Exhibition of 1878, does not seem to have quite determined on its style yet, and wavers between comic opera and comic drama.

These minor Parisian theatres have one peculiarity. On or about the first of January they often produce a piece chronicling and satirizing the events of the past year, and obviously called a "review" of the year. Mr. John Brougham endeavored to naturalize the review in New York when he opened his pretty little Fifth Avenue Theatre in 1869, but the attempt failed. A like result seems to have attended the several attempts of Mr. J. R. Planché, and the single attempt of Mr. H. J. Byron to carry the review across the Channel to England. Novelty of incident is necessary to cloak the similarity of plot. The opportunity the review offers for "local hits" and personalities is too tempting to be missed; but it has been so frequently abused, that, like the custom of producing pantomimes at Christmas in London, the practice of preparing a New Year's annual in Paris began slowly to die out about a decade ago. Within the past two or three years the fashion seems to be coming a little more into favor again.

It was for the late Charles James Mathews and his wife, Madame Vestris, that Mr. Planché made the attempt to transplant the review; and for their acting the dramatist did succeed in transplanting a great variety of lighter French plays. It was perhaps in return for these involuntary loans that

The Theatres of Farce and Extravaganza. 185

Mathews made two appearances in Paris. It may be remembered that Talma was always anxious to go over to London to play *Hamlet* in English, and that the late J. B. Booth, on one occasion at least, acted *Oreste* in French with a French company in New Orleans. Mathews went over to Paris in 1863 and acted at the Variétés in "L'Anglais Timide," a French play adapted by himself from the English "Cool as a Cucumber." His success was so great that he returned two years later to play "L'Homme Blasé," the piece from which the English "Used Up" had been taken.

It was at this same Variétés that the best and the best-known of M. Offenbach's opéra bouffes originally saw the light. The "Belle Hélène," the "Grand Duchess of Gérolstein," the "Périchole," and the "Brigands" are, musically, the most charming of the composer's works, and the librettos, by MM. Meilhac and Halévy, the authors of "Froufrou," are wonderfully clever. And it is evidence of the decadence into which opéra bouffe has now fallen, that, although the company at this theatre is headed by Mme. Judic, an actress of genuine comic power, who first made her name as a singer, and by M. Dupuis, the creator of *Paris*, and of *Fritz*, and of *Piquillo*, yet music plays only an incidental part in the pieces they act.

Leaving on one side the comic theatres which, like the Variétés, still allow a little music, there remain nearly half-a-dozen houses devoted to light comedy. The style of performance at these theatres may be said to resemble somewhat that once given here in New York at Mitchell's Olympic. It is not unlike that presented for nearly a score of years at the London Strand Theatre; and in so far as any theatre in this nation, still ruled by inherited Puritan prejudices, can be similar to a theatre in sensual and sensuous Paris, now as always under the reign rather of the impuritans, it may be said that the light and cheerful performances given at the Park Theatre in this city are akin in type to those to be seen at the Parisian minor houses of this class.

But due allowance must be made for the differences of national taste. In Paris the bill of fare is far more highly spiced. In Paris there are more mushrooms and more truffles. The public frequenting these little theatres demands simply to be amused, and the authors try to meet the demand. *Castigat ridendo mores* and *Veluti in speculo* are mottoes equally despised. Amusement is the sole aim of author and actor. The plays are rarely long, but they are often broad. The dramatist takes out a full poet's license, and his plays are at times as licentious as Ovid or Boccaccio. You are sure to be treated there to all the indelicacies of the season. Not only the words, but sometimes the ground-plan of the piece is not of a nature to be literally translated into polite English. The daughter cannot take her mother to the little theatre in the Palais-Royal; nor do you ever see there young ladies not married, either *de jure* or *de facto.* Innocent English families, ignorant of the freedom of speech existing there, frequently quit the theatre before the close of the performance, horrified. More than once have French authors, at a loss to raise a laugh, placed among the audience a party of actors caricaturing the English, who at a certain point blushingly rise and leave the house, murmuring " Shoking! shoking! "

The Palais-Royal originally opened with four decorous one-act comedies, which were all hissed. It then went to the other extreme. Its plays were the most risky, not to say reckless, in Paris. From the careful manner in which the morals of French girls are guarded, this theatre has all the flavor of forbidden fruit. It is longed for in silence, and ignorance of its real character but increases the thirst for knowledge. It is said that the first favor a young Parisian bride asks from her husband is to take her to the Palais-Royal Theatre. Of course, after a well brought up young woman discovers by personal experience that the plays sold in the Palais-Royal are no purer than the jewelry to be bought in the Palais-Royal, she rarely has any desire to increase her store of knowledge.

In Fielding's comedy " Pasquin," the dramatist,

Trapwit, describes a piece of his composing thus :—
" For to tell you the truth, sir, I have very little, if any, wit in this play ; no, sir, this is a play consisting of humor, nature, and simplicity ; it is written, sir, in the exact and true spirit of Molière ; and this I will say for it, that except about a dozen, or a score or so, there is not one impure joke in it."

Mr. *Trapwit's* play would have suited the stage of the Palais-Royal exactly. For nearly thirty years the Palais-Royal was one of the most successful theatres in Paris. It had a fine company and it produced clever pieces. But of late its luck has turned: its company seems to have lost its hold on the public, and a constant succession of plays has been brought out only to die a hasty death.

This change of fortune may be traced to two concurrent causes. The first is, that the people of Paris are tired of buffoonery. The body of the French populace ask for something stronger, better, more wholesome, leaving a cleaner taste in the mouth, than the fare offered at the Palais-Royal. The second is, that to those who yet like these highly spiced meats, other theatres are proffering a dish of still more gamey flavor. There is the Athenée, for instance, situated in a cellar in the Rue Scribe, and giving a performance even lower morally than its stage is actually. In short, the Palais-Royal is left between two stools: those of its old customers, who put up with its indecencies for the sake of its fun, will do so no longer, but have gone forth to seek more innocent enjoyment elsewhere; and those who were attracted to the Palais-Royal by that very indecency can now find more attractive entertainment at other theatres.

Unless a change occurs soon in the public temper, there may pass out of existence a theatre which began its career almost contemporaneously with the coming of the Second Empire, and which was in a measure the adequate reflection of the manners and morals of that epoch. The frivolity, the emptiness, the buffoonery, the scoffing at ties hitherto held sacred, and at opinions hitherto deemed honorable, the corruption, the greed, and the self-seeking which characterized the eighteen years of imperial misrule must bear their share of the responsibility for the existence of a theatre like the Palais-Royal. And the theatre was not without influence in creating the state of feeling which made the Commune possible, and which leads one of the French poets of the latest school to sum up all philosophy in a quatrain that might well be written on the walls of the Palais-Royal theatre:

> "Voilà ma vie, o camarade,
> Elle ne vaut pas un radis.
> Ça commence par une aubade,
> Ça finit en *De profundis*."

CHAPTER XII.

OTHER PLACES OF AMUSEMENT.

BESIDES the theatres and opera-houses which have been considered in the foregoing chapters; besides the theatres of less importance which of necessity have been omitted in a scant enumeration like this; and besides the local suburban theatres, of which there is one in nearly every one of the outlying wards of Paris, there are in the capital of France a great variety of other places of amusement.

First of all, there are no less than four circuses. The Cirque Fernando and the Winter Circus are only open in the cold months, while during the warmer weather the Summer Circus, in the Champs Elysées, and the Hippodrome, out toward the Trocadero hill, give nightly performances. These homes of equestrianism are not the temporary canvas edifices which spring up in the night, like mushrooms, all over the United States, during the long summer months, but solid and enduring buildings, either of brick and marble, like the Summer and Winter Circuses, or of iron, like the new Hippodrome. The Summer Circus in the Champs Elysées, is a fine, handsome building, adorned with equestrian statues.

One of the earliest circuses in Paris was built in 1780 by the famed Philip Astley, who founded the celebrated Astley's Circus in London. He was followed in time by Franconi. Astley was an Englishman, Franconi an Italian, and only recently Paris was delighted by a new American circus managed by Mr. Myers. In all countries an acrobat, like a musician, has to be a foreigner to be appreciated. In America the gymnasts, who are very often half-Germans, pretend to be Italians or Spaniards, and the riders, especially those of the fair sex, affect French names. In France the most popular acrobats and riders are Americans, while clowns are always English. The performances in the ring of any one of the Parisian circuses are not better than those offered to us in America by any one of our half-dozen best travelling companies. Indeed, they do not differ greatly, for the circus profits especially by the present cosmopolitanism of art, and all really good performers go frequently from one country to another. There is scarcely a first-rate acrobat or rider, whatever his nationality, who has not been seen in the arena in both Paris and New York. The only notable differences in the equestrian performances in the two cities are the result of the permanence of the buildings in Paris—a permanence which allows greater display and richer and more elaborate accessories.

More characteristic of Parisian life, and far more

frequent than the circuses, are the café-concerts, entertainments akin to the English "music-hall," and to the American "variety show," but still differing from either in many respects. As in England and America, the performance consists of a medley of songs and recitations, and little farces, and sometimes of juggling or acrobatics. But the French café-concert is rarely like a regular theatre, and very seldom has it any scenery. It is, in fact, a concert-hall, with a shallow stage at one end. At the rear of this stage, in a semicircle, sits a row of fair vocalists in full evening toilet, arranged much like the negro minstrels of our native land when the trouble is about to begin. These are the stock company, and from time to time one of them advances to the foot-lights and sings a song, sentimental or humorous, or of that more wearying variety known as "serio-comic." The star singers do not sit on the platform, but emerge from the side-scenes when their turn comes, which is always toward the end of the evening. The singers are accompanied by a little orchestra, in the usual place in front of the stage. At intervals a masculine vocalist comes forward, generally to inflict upon us an excruciating comic song of the kind which Mr. J. R. Planché has feelingly called "most music-hall, most melancholy."

Two or three times during the evening the ladies troop off, leaving the stage bare for a little dramatic piece, a farce, or vaudeville, or operetta. This will, in all probability, be followed by an exhibition of gymnastics, or of some sort of sensational dancing; after which the fair vocalists return to their seats, and the feast of music is resumed.

The great peculiarity of these café-concerts is, that the admission is free, but the spectator must give an order to one of the many waiters in attendance. You must either eat or drink for the good of the house. A cup of coffee or chocolate, an ice-cream, or a glass of beer—that will suffice. Of course the prices are higher than at an establishment where there is no music. You can get nothing for less than a fixed sum, varying from a half franc to a franc and a half, according to the class of seat you may have chosen. And you must " consume " something; for, as the sign reads, " the consumption is obligatory."

I remember wandering through the Exhibition of 1867 with a friend whom the world now knows as a poet who rhymes sonnets to strange exotic subjects, exhaling a peculiar and personal savor. We heard an odd humdrum thrumming, which, as we discovered at last, came from an Algerine café-concert. Curiosity took us up a little flight of circular stairs to a dirty and dingy room, at the end of which sat three prehistoric and preternaturally hideous Algerian women, one of whom was lazily strumming on some sort of a stringed instrument, while the other two languidly regarded us, the only other occupants of the room save the waiter. Our curiosity instantly sated, we turned and went speedily down the little stairs. But we were not at the foot before the waiter at the head called to the boss below : " These gentlemen have not consumed!" And we were fain to pay tribute, to avoid a "consumption" of more than doubtful cleanliness.

In a little hall upstairs in a building in the central line of the Boulevards is the theatre which was founded by the late Robert-Houdin, the greatest of all modern necromancers—if indeed he ever had his equal in ingenuity and skill. Performances of magic are given there every night, and on frequent afternoons for the benefit of the children, young and old, who delight in feeding on the marvellous. The theatre is now under the management of the son of Robert-Houdin.

There are in Paris some ten little marionette theatres, and they are not the least interesting of its dramatic amusements. Five of them, grouped together in the Champs Elysées, just opposite the Palais de l'Industrie, are familiar to every young American who has been to Paris. These theatres are of two kinds. They are either *jeux de triangle*, the actors being true marionettes, ingeniously articulated and skilfully moved by wires from above; or they are *jeux de castollet*, puppets of the familiar Punch-and-Judy type, animated from below by the inserted hand of the performer. The first kind are rarely seen in England and America, while even in Paris they are less popular. The typical French play in which they appear is the " Temptation of St. Anthony," full of peculiar spectacular sensations.

The second class, which we know in America by the English name of Punch-and-Judy, requires an outfit far less expensive, and indeed often portable. It is seen to advantage in the streets of German and Italian provincial towns, and, even in Paris, the protagonist is provincial: *Guignol* is a Lyonnais. Among the half-score of little puppet-theatres there can be no question as to the superiority of the Vrai Guignol in the Champs Elysées handled by M. Anatole, a most ingenious and inventive spirit, the author of his own half-extemporaneous plays, rarely twice alike ; the MSS. of several of which, now in my possession, go far to show that M. Anatole, like his predecessor as a playwright, the divine Williams, possesses a most variegated orthography.

A novel display of great interest to all students of the stage was to be seen at the Exhibition of 1878. The Ministry of Public Instruction, Religion, and the Fine Arts has a general supervision of the theatres, under the final clause of its title. This important department of the Ministry would not allow the Exhibition to pass without seizing the opportunity to make itself better known and to set forth as far as possible the history of the stage in France. A commission, including M. Garnier, the architect, and M. Halanzier, at that time the Manager of the Opéra, and M. Perrin, the manager of the Comédie-Française, was appointed; the result of its labors was to be seen in one of the little pavilions adjoining the long central picture-galleries.

Since the organization of the archives of the Opéra there has been gradually forming there a complete collection of the *maquettes* of the scenes of all operas produced there since 1864. A *maquette*, it may be as well to explain, is the miniature model, drawn to scale, which the scene painter prepares for submission to the manager and author, and to guide him in the execution of the full-sized painting. Selecting ten of the most effective and elaborate of the *maquettes* in the collection of the Opéra, fourteen others were reconstructed upon the same uniform scale (three centimetres to the metre) from engravings, sketches, descriptions, carrying the history of scenic decoration back from our time to the earlier days of the regular French stage. We were thus enabled to see the small stage of the Hôtel de Bourgogne, where, about 1619, was produced the " Folie de Clidamant, pièce de M. Hardy," the scenery for which is copied from a sketch in a MS. of the National Library (a MS. apparently of a stage-manager's note-book), wherein it is accompanied by this description : " There must be in the middle of the stage a fine palace, and on one side the sea, in which appears a vessel rigged with masts, on which a woman who throws herself into the sea, and on the other side a fine chamber which opens and shuts, where there is a bed well decked with cloths." From the *maquette*, as from this description, it seems that the rigidity with which the French bound themselves by the false rule of the unity of place was compensated, to some extent at least, by the liberality with which they endowed the chosen place with all needed qualities.

Other of the earlier scenes were scarcely less curious than this. From the original sketch of the artist, Pizzoli, a *maquette* was made of the scene of the third act of that "Psyché, tragédie-ballet," represented for the first time in 1671, and due to the collaboration of Corneille, Molière, and Quinault. After this, documents and sketches being wanting, there was an abrupt jump to the first years of this century, to the 13th Floréal, Year VIII., when a "Hécube" was produced at the Opéra with a terrific display of the sack of Troy. Then we came rapidly to scenes from the "Roi de Lahore," the latest opera which up to that time had been given on the stage of the Opéra.

But interesting as this collection of *maquettes* was, it was not as useful to the student of the stage as two other articles exhibited with it. The regular drama of France grew out of the early Mysteries; and in this theatric exhibition the *maquettes* of the modern theatre were accompanied by a reproduction, on the same scale (three centimetres to the metre), of the platform on which was performed the well-known Mystery of Valenciennes, three copies of which are in existence, each adorned with a painting representing the elaborate staging and comprehensive "set" of the scenery. From this painting the model was made, and nothing is more curious than the way in which all the possible places needed in the course of the Mystery were accumulated on one platform, from heaven, with some of its inhabitants, on the left, to hell, with several energetic devils, on the right; while in between were Nazareth, the Temple, Jerusalem, the palace of the high-priest, the Sea of Galilee with a boat in it, and the Golden Gate.

Side by side with this popular stage of the middle ages was the popular theatre of antiquity. The type chosen was the colossal Roman theatre of Orange, whose walls, though bare, are standing to this day. A model of this, on the same scale as the *maquettes*, was executed by M. Darvant, under the direction of MM. Garnier and Heuzey. The Orange Theatre is sixty-one metres wide, while the new Paris Opéra is only sixteen. The immensely greater size of the old theatre was shown by a glance at the surrounding *maquettes*, and also by a

Other Places of Amusement. 199

figure of an actor, made in due proportion and placed, a tiny speck in the proscenium. Copies of this model, protagonist and all, would be of great use in the study of the Greek tragedians in our American colleges.

These were the more important objects in the Theatric Exposition. The walls were covered with sketches of scenery and costumes drawn from the archives of the national theatres. Some of the earlier frames were very amusing : No. 27, " Opera Costumes of Time of Louis XV.," contained an Afriquain and an Afriquaine, and an Amérigain and an Amérigaine, the men being respectively black and brown, while their fair consorts were white ; all were adorned with abundant feathers, and there was but little difference between the Afriquain and the Amérigain.

CHAPTER XIII.

CONCLUSION.

THE relations of the newspapers and the theatres are, in Paris, close and cordial. There is a certain amount of jealousy between the journalists and the dramatists; but it is of slight importance, since nearly every writer in Paris of any prominence has at one time or another written for the stage. The theatres are always hospitable to the newspapers. At the Théâtre Français it is said that a journalist having once acquired a right to a specified seat as the dramatic critic of a newspaper, is ever afterward entitled to claim it on all first performances and similar solemnities, although his connection with the press may have ceased. During the presidency of M. Thiers a story was even told of a seat which a frequenter of the Théâtre Français had noticed vacant several times when he had vainly sought accommodation. At last he went to the clerk and demanded to know the name of the critic who had the right to the wished-for seat. The functionary looked at his books and read: "Stall 46. Service of the press. 1824. *Le Constitutionnel.* M. Adolphe Thiers!"

Conclusion. 201

In all the old-fashioned French newspapers there is a weekly review of the dramatic doings of the past seven days. In the Monday morning number, which generally comes out on Sunday evening, the *feuilleton*, as the daily instalment of the usual novel is called, is omitted, and its place on the ground floor of the newspaper is filled by a carefully considered dramatic criticism. In accordance with the custom of French journalism, these articles are signed by the name of the writer. To be the dramatic critic of an important paper, is held honorable. Among the well-known French authors who are now contributing signed dramatic criticisms every week to the papers of Paris, are MM. A. Daudet, Théodore de Banville, Émile Zola, Jules Claretie, Édouard Fournier, and Francisque Sarcey.

Some of the more fashionable and less instructive papers have abandoned the weekly dramatic review, and devote daily an increasing portion of their space to things theatrical. On the morning after M. Offenbach opened the Gaîté, in September, 1873, the *Gaulois* gave five columns to a description of the improvements in the theatre, and a detailed criticism of the performance of the preceding evening.

About one-sixth of the reading matter in the *Figaro* concerns the stage. At the foot of the fourth page (the *Figaro*, like all Parisian dailies, has the folio form) is the programme for that evening of each of the leading theatres, with the full cast of characters. This is changed from day to day, as at the Opéra, Opéra Comique, and Théâtre Français, even the most successful pieces are only performed two or three times a week, the other nights being devoted to revivals or plays kept permanently in the repertory. The *Figaro*, imitated by its immediate rivals like the *Gaulois*, marks distinctly the difference between the dramatic critic and the theatrical reporter. M. Auguste Vitu, a critic of singular discrimination, remarks upon every new play within forty-eight hours after its production. The *Figaro* has also a musical critic, who notices all concerts and operas. Besides these two critics there are also two reporters controlling on alternate days a column of stage news and gossip; it is their duty to chronicle the latest gossip about authors or actors; to give the cast of forthcoming pieces, and to mention all arrivals and revivals, dramatic and musical. There is also a pseudonymous writer, *le Monsieur de l'Orchestre*, who attends all first nights, and publishes the next morning a chatty description of the occupants of the boxes, the dresses of the ladies, the look of the house, the distinguished people present, noting any witty remarks made among the audience (inventing them if need be), and, in a word, giving in a few graphic and piquant paragraphs a lively account of all that took place before the curtain.

The career of a new comedy in a newspaper is something like this. It is mentioned in the column of theatrical gossip when it is accepted, when it is read, and when it is rehearsed; its cast appears in an advertisement on the fourth page of the papers on the day of its production; the *Monsieur de l'Orchestre*, or some similar writer, sketches the state of the house the next morning, and, the day after, the regular critic gives a careful analysis of play and players. And on the Monday following, all the heavy and respectable political sheets contain an elaborate and ably-expressed account of the new piece. Should it be a success, anecdotes of it, more or less true, will occasionally appear, indirectly advertising the play.

It has been suggested by an American writer that if William Shakespeare had been born in the nineteenth century, and had lived in these United States, he would have been the editor of a newspaper; while if he had been an Englishman he would have written novels. This may be doubted. But there can be no doubt that had he been a French man of our generation he would have stuck to his old trade, and made plays. In France the dramatic is still the foremost department of literature. In England the novel has claimed the attention of certainly four of the first literary intelligences of this century; the stage not one. In the United States we have contributed one, and possibly two great names to the history of prose fiction; but none to that of dramatic literature. In France the reverse is true: the French novelists are collectively and individually inferior to the French dramatists. The two foremost story-tellers, Victor Hugo and Alexandre Dumas, are even more renowned as playwrights. There is no contemporary French novelist to be compared for a moment with any one of the three fine writers now at the head of French dramatic literature—M. Émile Augier, M. Alexandre Dumas, and M. Victorien Sardou. Nearly one-fourth of the illustrious forty of the French Academy are dramatists.

In fact, in France, to-day, the way to both fame and fortune lies through the stage door. A play takes higher rank than a novel, and brings in more money. It is no more difficult to write, because the theories of dramatic construction seem to be possessed by a Frenchman almost intuitively, and because also the habit of collaboration makes it possible for the most inexperienced writer to get the aid of technical assistance. It is nearly as easy to dispose of; the path of the beginner, of course, is always hard, whatever the field he seeks to till. But in France the market for plays is large and open. The theatres of Paris, fifty of them more or less when we include the suburban houses, demand a constant supply of new dramas.

The French dramatist has now one great advantage over the dramatist of any other country: he has no foreign competition. Owing to the skill of French playwrights, their work has been exported to every civilized capital. In Germany and in England, the home product of plays is supplemented by imports from France, and it is fortunate for the English or German dramatist if the foreign article does not form the staple of consumption. In the United States the native dramatist has to compete as best he may with English plays and German plays, and, above all, with French plays.

Now the French dramatist knows nothing of these drawbacks. He has his market to himself. The Parisian play-goer likes the fare offered to him to have been prepared especially for him; he detests warmed-over dishes. I can recall only two foreign plays acted at Paris during the past year, 1879, one a German comic opera, and the other an Italian tragic drama. The French people have not yet even had a chance to hear the ubiquitous strains of "H. M. S. *Pinafore.*" In spite of all its cosmopolitanism, Paris shows no signs of any weakening in its affection for home-made plays.

The position of the manager of an important theatre in Paris is therefore very different from that of a New York manager, who, whenever he cannot put his hand at once on an American play of great promise, has only to pick and choose among the latest productions of the French, German, or English stage. The French manager has no such resource. He must rely on his own sagacity. He cannot buy his successes ready made for him. He has to judge for himself. He is not unreasonable; he does not expect every new play to succeed—or even every other new one. Like a wise publisher, the manager knows that there can only be an average of success. Just as one book pays cost, another is a loss, and a third brings in a good round profit, so one play may be damned at first sight, another may furnish forth a respectable career, while the third makes a fortune. If the proper proportion of plays meet with popular approval, the Parisian manager is satisfied. Nearly one hundred and fifty original pieces are brought out at the twenty leading theatres of Paris every year.

It is evident that the dramatic authors of France and the managers of the theatres of Paris could not continue this enormous productiveness, which increases from year to year, if they were not aided by competent criticism, and sustained by a fine popular taste in theatricals. The skill of the dramatic critics and the honorable dignity of their office may be judged from what has been said before in this chapter. The popular taste does not lag far behind. The Parisian play-goer has given up the right to applaud, but he retains the faculty of criticism, adverse or appreciative, as the case may be. It seems almost as though the French were born dramatic critics. They have the first element of criticism—a strong love for the subject. And they have also the second element—a willingness to analyze their impressions.

"In France," said Sainte-Beuve, "the first consideration for us is not whether we are amused and pleased by a work of art or mind, nor is it whether we are touched by it. What we seek above all to learn is, whether *we were right* in being amused with it, and in applauding it, and in being moved by it." And Mr. Matthew Arnold, who translates this passage, adds that, "These are very remarkable words, and they are, I believe, in the main, quite true. A Frenchman has, to a considerable degree, what one may call a conscience in intellectual matters; he has an active belief that there is a right and a wrong in them, that he is bound to honor and obey the right, that he is disgraced by cleaving to the wrong." The conscience that all the world has in moral matters, the Frenchman has in intellectual — and especially in literary matters. And it is this trait in his character which has given France in our day the foremost dramatic literature of the century.

Some may object that in proportion as the Frenchman gained a conscience in intellectual matters, he lost in morals. Well, no doubt, there is some excuse for the wide-spread belief in the immorality of French dramatic literature. There are even those who think of the manners and morals of the French stage, as Dr. Johnson thought of the manners and morals of my Lord Chesterfield's entertaining letters to his son. But this is at best a superficial view; and it results mainly, although, alas, not altogether, from the freedom French dramatists enjoy of treating any subject they may choose, provided only that their play be well done. "I know no immoral plays," says M. Dumas, "I only know ill-made plays." A French drama may discuss a deep social problem; it is not spoon-meat for babes, and a French theatre is no place for a young ladies' boarding-school.

It is also partly owing to this loosing of the shackles of conventionality that the French drama of to-day is as vigorous and virile as it is. Certainly no student of social science, no one who seeks to spy out the secret springs of French character, can afford to neglect the theatres of Paris. Taking them with the good and the bad, all in all, they are a mirror of French existence. As Lord Lytton wrote, in the "Parisians"—and the words are as true now as when written—"there is no country in which the theatre has so great a hold on the public as in France; no country in which the successful dramatist has so high a fame; no country, perhaps, in which the state of the stage so faithfully represents the moral and intellectual state of the people."

www.ingramcontent.com/pod-product-compliance
Lightning Source LLC
Chambersburg PA
CBHW021815230426
43669CB00008B/757